HOW TO
TEACH ADULTS

William A. Draves

Learning Resources Network

Cover design by Alan Edgar

Published by The Learning Resources Network (LERN), P.O. Box 1448, Manhattan, Kansas 66502.

Library of Congress Cataloging in Publication Data
Draves, Bill, 1949–
    How to teach adults.

    Bibliography: p.
    Includes index.
    1. Adult education.   2. Teaching   I. Title.
LC5215.D73   1984   374   83-82761
ISBN 0-914951-21-1
ISBN 0-914951-20-3 (pbk.)

Printing
5

"If you want to teach adults successfully and enjoyably, this is the book to have at hand." Ronald Gross, author of *The Lifelong Learner*

"A marvellously comprehensive and practical guide to teaching adults. Useful for frequent reference." Allen Tough, author of *The Adult's Learning Projects*

"A down to earth book dealing with reality. There are many specifics that will be helpful to the experienced practitioner as well as to the beginner." Leonard Nadler, author of *Developing Human Resources*

"A book which is useful to all adult education teachers—beginning and experienced. Draves writes in a very readable style with jargon-free language." Donald W. Mocker, in *The Adult Learning Review of Books*

To Susan Warden

à la danse de ma vie

TABLE OF CONTENTS

Acknowledgments

As a journalist in adult learning, I am indebted first to those who have made this story: teachers, past and present; including those who have taught me, those I interviewed for this book, and those, like Russell Robinson and Malcolm Knowles, who have written about their experiences from which I have drawn heavily for the book.

My appreciation goes to those who have contributed to this book, including: Sue Bacon, my copy editor, for her pen, critique, and coaching during the manuscript's three years of development; Michael Collins, Ronald Gross, and A. Jean Lesher, for their enthusiasm and encouragement; William A. Draves III for the index and corrections; Glenna Wilson for help with proofreading; Carolyn Arand and Deb Quinn for production help; and to Susan Warden for her support and her example of a teacher par excellence.

Chapter 1
Introduction

One day Karen Thiel was teaching her "Life Work Planning" class at the technical institute in Fond du Lac, Wisconsin. In the middle of the class a woman mistakenly walked into her classroom. Instead of leaving, the woman was captivated by the exercises the class was doing, and then joined in them.

At the end of the class, the woman told Mrs. Thiel, "It's been very fascinating, and very enjoyable, but next week I'm going to *have* to go to my creative writing class."

You too can teach a class so interesting that even a person who is supposed to be somewhere else will find it exciting.

This book will help you teach adults in a group or classroom setting. It was written to provide you with proven techniques for preparing, conducting, and improving your class. You may be new to teaching adults, and see this as an introduction to lifelong learning. Or you may have taught adults before, and want to continue learning about teaching by incorporating new ideas.

After reading this book, you will gain new insights into helping adults learn, pick up tips on different teaching techniques, and be able to evaluate your experience better. In doing so, you will make your teaching more stimulating.

A Different Kind of Teacher

Welcome to the learning explosion. People are interested in learning just about anything these days, from practical skills like repairing a toaster to philosophical issues about Zen and life after death. The range of topics is unlimited, from the outer reaches of the universe to the inner workings of the brain. We are now in a world in which a person can study just about any imaginable topic.

No longer are people content to sit back and say, "I have my education," but instead are making learning a lifelong pursuit. This has meant a new era for teaching as well, with different approaches and techniques for helping adults learn. It has called for a different kind of teacher, one who understands how adults learn, one who can create a positive climate for learning, tap the experiences and talents of the students themselves, and one who is also a lifelong learner and wants to improve his own facilitating of adult learning.

In fact, in this new era adult learning is no longer limited to adults. Rather, an "adult learner" is one who chooses to be in a given learning situation. Thus, the term "adult learners" refers to people of all ages, including teenagers and even children when they voluntarily participate in a group learning activity or class.

To respond to the needs of today's adult learner, thousands of people are teaching who have never done so before. Their entrance into teaching is not as a teacher but as someone with a particular skill or knowledge of a subject he wants to share. Some of these new teachers, teaching part-time for relatively modest reimbursement, do not even think of themselves as teachers. They are joined by professional teachers, people who have been trained to teach for a living, but for whom teaching adults is somewhat different from previous formal instruction. They all have in common the desire to share what they know with others.

We want to teach because we have a need to share knowledge. There are two reasons for this. First, we know more now. Every person has a wealth of information and skills to offer others. And secondly, there are fewer avenues or ways to tutor or teach others. In past decades, we passed on ideas through the family, the church, civic groups, and other organizations. Today participation in these institutions is declining, and thus opportunities to teach through these organizations are also fewer. Although we know more, there are fewer channels for conveying that knowledge. Consequently, the opportunity to share one's own knowledge with other adults in a class setting is an inviting one for many people like yourself.

The tradition of people teaching others is long. Although professional teachers have always had a place in our society, we tend

2

to forget that "lay" teaching has a rich history as well. One hundred years ago, there were fewer colleges as compared with today. Yet people learned, and they learned from each other. Fathers taught their sons a trade; mothers taught their daughters homemaking skills. Skilled laborers took on apprentices. And there were libraries, Lyceums, Chautauquas, Extension, and other places to teach adults. Later, adults taught others in Sunday School, as scout leaders, in civic organizations, and in professional associations. Your opportunity to teach and the knowledge we possess about teaching adults has grown out of those traditions of adults teaching adults.

This new learning explosion is occurring predominantly in the class or group setting—two or more people led by a facilitator or teacher. Within that common format, the learning is varied in its location, subject, and sponsorship. It is taking place in formal classrooms, in living rooms, in work places and the office, in large lecture halls, in parks, and even in restaurants and taverns. Many of these classes are noncredit; some are for credits, continuing education units or certificates; but all are taking place because adults want to learn.

All kinds of organizations are participating: colleges and universities, community colleges and technical institutes; public schools; city recreation agencies; learning networks and free universities; employers, businesses and corporations; civic, community and voluntary organizations; social agencies, mental health centers, hospitals; and independent centers. In addition, many unaffiliated individuals are offering courses independently.

Why You Should Read This Book

Why should you read part or all of this book? Because teaching adults is difficult, and the learning situation is fragile. The importance of knowing the information in this book is critical. It can make the difference between a successful class and an unsuccessful one.

The chapters of the book show you how to plan better, teach, and improve your class. But they will also show you how to turn teaching from a chore into a joy. You can help others learn, and that is one of life's more rewarding experiences. Wherever you are teaching, you can turn the classroom or living room into a learning room. If you are enthusiastic, your students will have fun learning and learn more.

Little things can turn teaching from a chore into a joy. Just changing the title of the course altered the attitude of Reeta Grover, a Columbus, Ohio, policewoman who "had" to teach a course on careers for women in public safety. When administrator Margareth Anschild helped her reword the course title from "Women in Police Careers" to "It's Not a Crime to Apply," Officer Grover remarked, "This changed my whole outlook. Now I'm looking forward to teaching the course."

You may want to read the whole book, skim it, or read those parts most useful to you. Basically three aspects are covered in the book. The first is how adults learn and how you can help them learn better. The second is how to prepare for your class. The third contains various tips and ideas for teaching and improving your teaching techniques.

Almost all of the suggestions come not from the author, but from the deep and varied experiences of teachers, learners, and educators over a long period of time. They have been culled from other books, from articles, from personal conversations, and from actual class sessions to make this a book of commonly understood principles about teaching adults.

An Invitation To Teach

This is your invitation to teach. To join in one of the more important functions in life, passing on knowledge and skills to others. It is an activity that has taken place in doorways and on street corners, in academies and under marble columns—from Socrates to modern-day teachers, media commentators, independent scholars, and those who teach by doing.

It is both an opportunity and a responsibility. It is an opportunity for you to grow, to learn more, to gain a valuable skill that will help you in your work, career advancement, personal relating to others, self-esteem, and feeling of worth. It is an opportunity to meet and enjoy people. But it is also a responsibility to your learners to create the kind of climate in which they will feel comfortable, secure, and able to learn. A charge to demonstrate to them that you know they are not there to hear you pontificate or soak up your words of wisdom, but to internalize and be responsible for their own learning. A duty not so much to teach as to help them learn; to inspire them and encourage their innate desire to learn. To help them achieve whatever goal they have set for themselves. And to foster additional learning.

Chapter 2
How Adults Learn

"A teacher must be a learner himself. If he has lost his capacity for learning, he is not good enough to be in the company of those who have preserved theirs."
—Harry Overstreet

When twelve people walk into your class for the first time, each one will come already equipped with various experiences, attitudes, perceptions, and ideas. Each person will organize his or her thoughts differently, and each will be able to absorb new knowledge and ideas in his or her own way.

The adult's mental learning state is not a blank chalkboard on which you, the teacher, can write as you wish. Neither is the adult learner's head an empty pail for you to fill with your knowledge and ideas. The adult learner's chalkboard already has many messages on it, and his mental pail is almost full already. Your job as teacher is not to fill a *tabula rasa*, but to help your participants reorganize their own thoughts and skills. A prerequisite to helping adults learn is to understand how they learn.

As complex human beings, we bring to the learning situation a combined set of emotional, physical, mental, and social characteristics that make each one of us unique. The way to approach this diversity in learners is with variety in your teaching. To do that, it is best to understand some of these characteristics of adults.

Emotional Characteristics

Adults' emotional states are inextricably tied up in their ability

7

to learn. To learn, an adult must be emotionally comfortable with the learning situation. Indeed, some educators have gone so far as to equate a good emotional state with learning. Says J. Roby Kidd in *How Adults Learn*, "Feelings are not just aids or inhibitors to learning; the goals of learning and of emotional development are parallel and sometimes identical and can probably be most conveniently stated as self-realization and self-mastery."[1]

Throughout the ages, one's emotional state has always been manipulated to try to induce learning, but somehow the attempt to produce positive feelings became distorted in the mistaken belief that greater learning would occur if one produced negative feelings of pain, fear, or anxiety.

The dunce cap, a sign of humiliation, was not originally intended to be so. Instead, the cone-shaped headgear was believed to have magical powers, just as some contemporaries believe the similar pyramid shape has unknown powers. Putting the cap on one who had missed a question or needed help was not a punishment, but was believed to help that person learn. Over the years the symbolism changed from a positive helping gesture to a sign of humiliation and ignorance.

Unfortunately vestiges of the punishment principle either consciously or unconsciously are present in even the most enlightened classes. Learning can be inhibited by frowns and other gestures.

In helping a person learn, the teacher must be able to help create a positive emotional climate, and the key to that state is one's *self-image*.

Although most adults come to a class mentally ready to learn, at the same time they may be inhibited from learning by a poor self-image. That poor self-concept may not be correct, may not be rational, but nevertheless exists in many people. It comes from various sources.

A shy person may feel unable to participate to meet the expectations of others in the class. A manager who has been turned down for several promotions may feel trapped in a dead-end job and doubt the value of learning anything. A housewife who has stayed at home with children for many years may feel she is not current or informed enough to converse on an "adult level" again. Someone who has been out of school for several decades may feel incapable of studying any more and may fear being left far behind the other students. The causes of a less than positive self-image are

8

many. They stem from natural feelings about inadequacy and growing older and some that are induced artificially by society.

Physical Characteristics

Abraham Lincoln may have been able to read at night by firelight, and children may have learned in straight-backed wooden desks in drafty log cabin schools, but today's adults can detect and be influenced by the slightest changes in comfort. Adults are more attuned to comfortable surroundings, more sensitive to discomfort.

Make sure your setting is comfortable, neither too warm nor too cold. Older people chill more easily, and your sense of warmth may not coincide with that of your group. In a small crowded room, your participants will become hot and stuffy sitting next to each other sooner than you will. Ask your participants to tell you if they are uncomfortable.

All adults in your class, even the younger ones, are declining physically. Everyone is aging, even those who refuse to admit it. Our physical state affects our capacity to learn. Physique and intelligence are related because our bodies influence how and whether we can learn.

To compensate for visual difficulties of learners of all ages, think carefully about how you can make words, charts, objects— even yourself—clear to all your participants.

Set up your room so that no one has to look directly into sunlight. If you use a chalkboard, use one that does not have glare. Make sure there is enough overhead lighting. Consider a flip chart instead of a chalkboard, and use large letters when writing on it. Seat people so they can see each other. Participants will engage in discussion and learn more from each other if they can see each other.

Just as important as seeing well is hearing well. Inability to hear well, either because of one's own capability or because of the setting, can make learners feel insecure, less intelligent, isolated, and far less willing to participate.

In preparing your class, think about how you can ensure that every participant will hear you. Try to select a room that is reasonably free of outside street noises, or noises from other rooms in the same building. Listen for any interference from heating sources, air conditioners, coffee pots, and any other systems or appliances in the room.

Design your space so that you can always be heard by your participants and so that they can hear each other. If you have a large class, experiment to see if a microphone helps or hinders. Speak in clear, loud, and distinct tones. Don't talk to your group with your back turned to them or while you are concentrating on something else, like setting up some projection equipment. Ask as often as you need to whether people in the back can hear you. When others in the class are talking, make sure they are facing the majority of the class. Ask people to stand up if necessary. Repeat questions from the group so everyone can hear them.

Mental Characteristics

Although adults may come to the learning situation with bodies that are not always in prime shape, the story is different for their mental attitudes. Mentally, adults are eager to learn—otherwise they would not be there.

Several aspects of adult learning mentality relate to your helping them to learn: a readiness to learn, problem orientation, and time perspective.

A *readiness to learn*. Adults for the most part will come to your class ready to learn. Almost all adult learning is voluntary these days, and even societal coercion, such as peer pressure, does not seem to affect adult learners. They attend because they want to.

Part of that readiness may be a natural growth process in which "true learning"—self-study, personal inquiry, or self-directed learning—is more welcome after one's formal schooling or education ends. Even the sixteenth century master of self-study, Montaigne, wrote about his education, "At thirteen . . . I had completed my course, and in truth, without any benefit that I can now take into account."[2] Whether their experiences in school were beneficial or not so positive, adults want to view their adult learning experiences as separate from more formal schooling, and will approach them differently. This may be because adults are not only ready to learn but need to learn.

Problem orientation. Education for children is often subject-centered, concentrating on various disciplines like philosophy and science, and the abstract as well as the practical. Adult learning, on the other hand, is more problem-centered. Adults want to learn to solve or address a particular problem, and are more satisfied with their learning if it applies to their everyday experiences, is practical, or is current.

Adults are oriented toward problem-solving because they are faced with certain developmental tasks stemming from the roles they assume, or want to assume, in their families, work, and society. These tasks and roles demand a good deal of adjustment, accomplishment, and learning. Although society pushes few adults into the classroom, it certainly creates enough needs and wants to encourage adults to perform their best in various roles and life stages.

Another and related impetus for problem-orientation in adult learning is that an adult's *time perspective* is different from that of children. As a child, time, both past and future, is a vast quantity. A year ago is a long time. And the future is endless. Increasingly as one becomes older, time becomes less expendable and more limited. The future is not so endless after all, and the past blurs a little so that ten years wasn't all that long ago. As time becomes more limited, it becomes more important. In the learning situation, adults prefer what can be learned today or in the near future to what can be learned over a longer period of time. The adults' interest in solving problems within their older time perspective makes adults more concerned with specific, narrow topics of relevance than broad, generalized or abstract subjects.

A readiness to learn, problem orientation, and specific time perspective contribute to an internal motivation to learn.

The time and problem orientations do not imply that everything adults want to learn is so immediate as fixing the plumbing. Many different kinds of issues, thoughts, and ideas may constitute a timely problem. For one person, finding out whether "beauty" lies in a museum painting or in a mountaintop view may constitute a legitimate learning problem. For another person determining how the ancient philosophers combined work with study may be an equally immediate problem.

Social Characteristics

The most important social characteristic of the adult learner is an abundance and variety of *experiences*. This aspect alone makes teaching adults different from teaching children or youth.

Your participants will be coming from different backgrounds, occupations, types of upbringing, ethnic heritages, and parts of

11

town. Each one will have a different mix of experiences and previously formed perceptions when entering your class. Some of these perceptions are about school, group interactions, and the subject.

School. Even if you are not working in a school-like atmosphere, structured learning situations are inevitably associated with previous schooling. For many people their formal schooling was less than successful. Many adults received low grades in school and have some stigma attached to that period of time. Others may have outwardly done well in school, but inwardly felt the experience was boring or a waste of time. Generally speaking, it is best to reduce the number of associations with formal schooling in your references, style, and approach to the subject. When teaching those with unfavorable school experiences, it is wise not to repeat those mannerisms and actions which may remind your participants of their past situations. The imprint of our schooling is still on all of us, and if those memories are not good, it is best not to revive them.

Group interactions. Your class is just one kind of group adults participate in. Some will come with positive expectations about interacting in a group; some will not. Some will come wanting to be leaders in the group; others will have already decided before the class starts to be passive or take a minimal role in group participation. Some will see the group as an opportunity to display talent and knowledge while others will see it as a possible threat to exposing their lack of talent and knowledge.

The subject. Every adult coming to your class will have some perception about the subject to be discussed. Some will have a degree of proficiency in the topic; others will have been acquainted more superficially. Some will have had a negative encounter with the topic, or gained some misinformation. Others will have thought about it from a distance, but come with curiosity and some ideas not based on reality but on what others have said or done.

Social psychologist Gardner Murphy says that adults, contrary to common assumption, are not able to detach themselves emotionally from the subject at hand. "The adult has not fewer but more emotional associations with factual material than do children although we usually assume that he has less," he says.[3]

Working with your participants' experiences is perhaps your most rewarding challenge. These varied and copious experiences need to be handled on two levels. First, you as a teacher need to deal with the backgrounds your participants bring to class. If someone has a negative image of schooling, you may have to help that person see this situation as different from past schooling. If a person in the group has gained some misinformation about the subject, you will need to clarify the misinformation. If some of your participants automatically shy away from participating in a group, you may want to try to draw them out or structure exercises to give them as much interaction as your overeager students have.

On another level, you have an abundant resource at hand in the past experiences of class members. Each has some event, skill, idea, or knowledge worth sharing with the rest of the group. You can tap into the variety in backgrounds to illustrate your points, to encourage discussion, to stimulate peer teaching, to gain new knowledge yourself. It is this wealth in your participants that makes teaching adults so exciting and rewarding. Drawing on your participants' experiences can make the class an exciting and new interaction every time you teach; to ignore those pasts is to miss out on something valuable and special.

The total of one's mental, emotional, physical and social states determines a person's motivation to learn. Much attention throughout history has been paid to how to motivate people. Generals have tried to motivate troops, supervisors have tried to motivate workers, salespeople have tried to motivate themselves, staffs have tried to motivate boards of directors, and boards of directors have tried to motivate staffs.

The quest for motivation has led to much thought on the subject as well. There is Theory X, Theory Y, and in the early 80s Americans imported Theory Z from Japan. Those writing about the power of positive thinking can stay on the best seller list for weeks or even years, and those speaking about it can fill halls with rallies on motivation.

It is still open to question whether you can directly motivate someone else, whether you can help motivate another, or whether you are powerless to influence a person's self-motivation. As a teacher, you will doubtless be confronted by people with a range of motivations, from those so highly motivated you will be reluctant to give them your home phone number, to those who will seem inert and lifeless and unreceptive to anything you say or any way you say it. How much time you want to devote in your course to stimulating motivation, and how you want to deal with the still inscrutable subject of motivation is up to you.

A few things are certain, however. One is that it is ultimately the individual's responsibility to learn. Another is that you as the teacher can help or hinder another person's attempts to learn. By failing to recognize limits, by ignoring or even constructing barriers, by not understanding how a person learns, you can be a negative influence on someone's learning. By facilitating learning and helping your participants, you can be a positive influence.

How Adults Learn. For Further Reading:

1. *How Adults Learn*, by J. Roby Kidd, Association Press, New York, 1979.
2. *The Adult Learner: A Neglected Species*, by Malcolm Knowles, Gulf Publishing Company, Houston, 1973.
3. *Adult Psychology*, by Ledford J. Bischof, Harper & Row Publishers, New York, 1969.

Chapter 3
Helping Adults Learn

"Those having torches will pass them on to others."
—Plato

Gilford Highet in *The Art of Teaching* retells the story of the famous orchestra conductor Toscanini who once arrived on tour in a new city and took over an orchestra he had never conducted before. He started conducting and after a minute or two noticed that the first violin player looked odd. He was playing well enough, but his face was all distorted, and when he turned a page of the score, he grimaced as though he were in great pain.

Toscanini stopped the orchestra and said, "Concert-master! Are you ill?" The first violin's face at once returned to normal.

"No, thank you," he said, "I'm quite all right, maestro. Please go on."

"Very well, if you're sure you're fit," Toscanini said. "Begin at D, please gentlemen." And off they went again. But the next time Toscanini glanced at the first violin, he saw him looking worse than ever. His face was all drawn up to one side, his teeth were showing between wolfish lips, his brow was furrowed with deep clefts, he was sweating painfully and breathing hard.

"One moment, please. Concert-master, you really look ill. Do you want to go home?"

"No, no, no, Mr. Toscanini, please go ahead."

"But I insist," said Toscanini. "What's wrong, are you having an attack, would you like to lie down for a while?"

"No, I'm not ill," said the first violin.

"Well, what on earth is the matter?" said Toscanini. "You look awful, you have been making the most agonizing faces, you're obviously suffering . . ."

"To be quite frank," said the first violin, "I hate music."

To teach well, one must enjoy it. This is simply a logical extension of the concept that learning is pleasurable. Once viewed as a heretical notion, the idea that learning should be as enjoyable as possible is now becoming more widespread. As the educator Kenneth Eble says, "I hold to one of the oldest views of nature, that learning is fun."[1] And if learning is to be fun, teaching must be enjoyable as well.

As we saw in the previous chapter, adults are self-motivated, interested, and usually eager to participate. Teaching adults, then, is not so much trying to convince, cajole, or tutor, as it is helping adults learn.

In fact, recently people have been trying to coin a term other than "teacher" to describe the person who helps adults learn, including trainer, facilitator, manager of the learning environment, resource person, group leader, and convener. Until another term replaces it, we shall stay with the word "teacher," but do so recognizing that the teacher of adults needs a different set of attributes, skills, and understandings.

The teacher of adults must have empathy, interest, and a feeling for people and teaching as much as the expertise in the subject being covered. Knowing what not to do is as important as what to do in teaching adults.

People are not necessarily born with good teaching traits. The great orator may be born, the genius may be born, but adults can learn to teach other adults. There are good teachers, of course, and poor ones, but all teachers can improve.

Attributes of a Good Teacher

We can describe the most commonly accepted characteristics of what makes a teacher of adults effective. But the descriptions will be general, and denote attitudes and basic skills. It may even leave you a bit unsatisfied; and that is simply because there is no one *way* to teach adults.

This author, like most of you, can recall having learned something on a snowy evening around a cabin fireplace while chatting with another person; and having learned just as much while sitting in a straight-backed high school desk in a classroom with a former West Point instructor lecturing. You will undoubtedly remember, as we list some of the favorable characteristics of adult teachers, equally outstanding teachers who didn't have a sense of humor, didn't care at all about the students or listen intently, and yet they excelled in teaching.

Nevertheless, it helps to talk about the kind of teacher people respond to most of the time. Even if you cannot develop every skill to the fullest—if you are sincere about becoming a good teacher—you probably will succeed. One of the chief characteristics of adult learners is that they appreciate and sympathize with someone who is trying.

Educator Frank C. Pearce describes the ideal teacher of adults as "people-centered, more interested in people than things, more interested in individuality than conformity, more interested in finding solutions than in following rules. The teacher must have understanding, flexibility, patience, humor, practicality, creativity and preparation."

One must meet three requirements before being able to teach adults:

—a love for your subject;

—a desire to share it; and

—a basic competence in the subject.[2]

The first two requirements are essential, but are best put simply. The last requirement has intimidated many potentially good teachers of adults because they have mistaken a "basic competence" for exceptional competence. Although there is little doubt that the more one knows about a subject, the more one can share, most people underrate their competence rather than overrate it. If you have a basic competence and are honest about your skills and experience in describing the course, by all means teach.

In evaluating classes, the problem most students point to *least* is the teacher's knowledge of the subject. Most student complaints come not from the teacher's knowledge of the subject but the teacher's ability to share that knowledge.

Furthermore, teachers of adults by far acquire their competence by doing and experience. Credentials play a minor part in the teacher's credibility and the students' interest in one's teaching ability. The old saying, "He who can, does; he who cannot, teaches" just doesn't hold true for teaching adults. In most adult learning, it is

17

the person who can who does the teaching.

Now let us look at some skills and steps to good teaching.

Skills You Should Have

Some general skills or talents apply to any teaching situation. Here are a few basic skills you should have or develop for the best possible teaching experience.

Listening. Listening is as important as effective speaking. And it is important to effective teaching because much learning takes place when a participant is expressing an idea. The attention a student receives when speaking can encourage his or her learning and interest, or inhibit it. A teacher can listen and encourage the student speaking by some sort of acknowledgment, either a verbal "uh-huh," or "I see" or nonverbal cues, such as a nod or smile. And a teacher can stimulate more discussion with what are called "door openers," such as "Would you like to talk about it?" or "Would you like to say more?"

Educator Russell Robinson, in *Helping Adults Learn and Change*, says the listener should:

- try to understand what is meant, not get ready to reply, contradict or refute;
- not interpret too quickly what the speaker is saying;
- put aside his own views;
- not jump ahead of the speaker;
- not prepare his answer while listening;
- be interested and alert and show it;
- not interrupt;
- expect the speaker's language to be different from his own;
- provide feedback;
- avoid negative feedback.[3]

Helping insecure learners. Learners who lack confidence in themselves are common in adult learning. A good teacher needs to make the learning environment secure for these people. Building their confidence is not condescending, but keeps their desire to learn alive.

In adult learning, enhancing security promotes learning. One of the ways to encourage the unconfident learner is through reward. That reward can be verbal reinforcement. Or it can be a smile, nod, or even occasionally a physical expression such as a handshake, pat on the back, touch on the arm, or hug.

Sometimes learners will demean themselves, professing inadequacy, frustration, or outside interference. When the learner is unhappy about some situation, focus on how the student *feels* about the external situation, not the situation itself. When someone begins personal demeaning, you should do the following:

—don't contradict the person's views;

—don't use logical explanations;

—don't ridicule that person's views;

—do convey your positive regard for the person.[4]

Wrong Things. One of the skills a teacher needs to develop is handling situations in which the learner is doing something wrong. Here are some "wrong" situations and how to correct them.

1. When the other person is doing the wrong thing,

—don't talk to the person, talk to the condition;

—describe what you see;

—describe what you feel;

—describe what needs to be done;

—say nothing to the person about himself.[5]

2. Some students prefer to be quiet and learn that way. Privacy deserves respect, but there are some overtures you as the teacher can make without intruding. Patience, invitations to speak, and other strategies, like dividing into subgroups or games, may involve quiet learners without embarrassing them.

3. "You" messages are bad, especially when things are not going right. Robinson says to avoid saying things like "You must," "you should," "you do it now," "you always," "you never," or "you act like . . ."

Instead, "I" messages are less offensive, and help turn the situation around. Say "I'm frustrated by this noise," or "I'm really annoyed when people interrupt me."[6]

4. When the adult learner does something wrong, don't punish that person, verbally or nonverbally. Adult educators are unanimous in their disapproval of punishment and negative reinforcement. It is counterproductive to learning. Punishment has inhibited more learning in a person's lifetime, and indeed throughout history, than any other single factor.

We can't say it strongly enough. Don't punish.

Supportive Actions. Certain words, phrases, gestures, or actions will go far in building a supportive atmosphere in which your participants will feel able to grow, learn, and respond to the

group and your leadership. Try:
—a smile
—responding to a raised hand
—a pat on the shoulder
—an expression of enthusiasm
—genuine pleasure at seeing your participants again
—listening with patience
—warm attentiveness to others
—helping a student with difficulty.

It may seem repetitive, but adult students learn best when they feel secure, and supportive words will build that security.

Humor. Although few of us are stand-up comics, many situations in the class will prompt a laugh or a smile. Take advantage of them, and use them well. Humor is good therapy. It puts people at ease, allows them to relax a little, and tensions disappear. Humor helps promote learning.

Here are some tips on using humor effectively.

a) Don't be afraid to use a joke if it is appropriate and is not overdone. Even a poor joke will be recognized as a good try.

b) Allow and encourage a little laughter and good fun. Don't stifle it unless it gets out of hand. There are usually pleasant and humorous situations in the class, and the teacher can take the lead in laughing a little at them.

c) Laugh at yourself. Laughing at others is hardly positive, but you can afford to point to one of your mistakes and invite the others to enjoy it.

d) If someone else in the class has the gift of humor, you can play off it or invite a comment or two from time to time.

e) If you don't have a knack for humor, don't try to force it. Smile a lot, be cheerful and pleasant, and just as much goodwill can flow from that.

Steps in Positive Teaching

From the beginning of your class through the end, you want to build and then maintain what is called a "positive learning climate," an atmosphere in which your students feel comfortable, are both part of the group and maintain their own individuality, respect and enjoy your leadership and the talents of the other members of the class, and are able to learn through positive reinforcement and caring.

There is no one correct way to build that climate; each teacher must do it his or her own way. If you are yourself, being honest, positive, interested in others, and friendly, you can set the tone. By carefully bringing in each member of the group, trying to recognize each participant in some way, you can create a good group. By welcoming dissent or disagreement and individual expression, you can enhance individuality. By reward and positive reinforcement—rather than emphasizing error and mistake—you can promote learning and the stimulus to learn. In these ways a positive climate is built, one in which you can teach, and they can learn.

In *Yes, You Can Teach*, Florence Nelson outlines the four steps of encouragement to maintain the learning climate throughout the class. Encouragement is not always effusive praise. Providing encouragement can be a subtle art, and it is a changing process depending on the needs of the learner. Nelson points to a four-step process that helps the learner become self-directed while lessening the role of the teacher. It illustrates that the best teachers are those who can step aside when the learner is ready.

These are the four steps of encouragement.

1. The fundamentals. In the beginning, effusive praise like "great," "wonderful," "keep going."
2. Pleasing you the teacher. As they advance, let them know, "It is coming along well," "Now you've got the right idea," and so on.
3. Pleasing you and themselves. Still further along, with comments like "Yes that's it . . . how do you feel about it?" or "I can see some progress here, what do you think?" or "I'll bet you're proud of yourself."
4. Pleasing themselves. And finally, when the learner is well along, you can step aside and say, "When you need help, just let me know."[7]

Helping Adults Learn. For Further Reading:
1. *The Art of Teaching*, by Gilbert Highet, Vintage Books, New York, 1950.
2. *The Craft of Teaching*, by Kenneth Eble, Jossey-Bass, San Francisco, 1976.
3. *Pedagogy of the Oppressed*, by Paulo Freire, Herder and Herder, New York, 1972.

Chapter 4
Preparing the Course

"It is a very tricky business, teaching."
—Gilford Highet

Every course needs preparation. Without it, your thoughts will be disjointed, the course structure fragmented, and the students will feel as though—well, you hadn't prepared. The dangers of underpreparation are many. You can forget points. You can give details out of sequence and confuse your students. You can talk too long and not leave time for other important topics. You can forget a visual aid or handout which would have helped in your presentation.

Teaching is not just talking. Even though you may know the subject thoroughly, a lack of preparation will make you look as if you don't know what you are talking about. Teachers have thought they could go into a situation and just start talking. Ideas would flow spontaneously because they know the subject so well. It just doesn't happen that way. Just as all those 'ad lib' jokes you hear comedians 'spontaneously' come up with are on index cards somewhere in a joke file, your remarks should be planned as well for maximum effect. Other teachers have thought they would sit down and say, "Well, what do you want to talk about?" and let the students ask questions to get the ball rolling. But students rarely can start asking questions about a topic they have not thought about before and the chances of this latter tactic working are slim.

Every course takes preparation. If you have taught the course before, it might take less preparation, but you still need to think about your next class as unique. If you have taught the course several times, you may need to prepare to make it different from others, to avoid becoming stale and conveying the "yellowed lecture notes"-feeling students have when they think the teacher has repeated it too often.

Goals, Objectives, and End Results

Before looking at each meeting separately, take a broad look at the course as a whole. What are the goals, objectives, and end results of the class?

Goals. Goals are long-term wishes. They are the reason you are teaching but are not necessarily achievable by the end of the course. The goal of a class on twentieth century painting may be a greater appreciation of art, and the goal for a class on investing wisely may be to help make the students financially independent. But neither goal is likely to be accomplished in the short time you are meeting. Look at your goals for the class. What do you want to happen in the class? Are the class goals consistent with your reasons for teaching this course in the first place? If they are not you need to revise the course. If you are not satisfied with the course goals your students will feel the negative effect.

Second, what would be a learner's goal in taking the class? Your students are time-conscious and problem-oriented, and perhaps their goals for the class may differ from yours. Their goals may not be an appreciation for art, but enough knowledge to get through the Louvre on their next trip to Paris. Their goals might not be financial independence, but doubling their current savings accounts. Teacher and learner goals are not incompatible and you need to think about their goals and perspective when you plan the course. By achieving the learner's goals you might just achieve yours as well.

The ideal way to meet your learners' goals is to sit down with them before the class starts and invite them to help plan the course with you. As you learn their goals for the class you then can go back and prepare the course with their specific needs and interests in mind. If you ever have the opportunity to plan your course with the students take advantage of this experience. Unfortunately, most classes need to begin when the students first come together and the course must be planned in advance. For most groups, you have to plan ahead with the students in mind, and then revise the course next time when you learn more about the students' needs.

Some preparing and revising can be done with the students, mostly on the "modification" level rather than on overall goals and the broader outline. The teacher should seek the students' help in the first session or even others, and then try to adjust somewhat to meet those particular interests and needs. By taking even five minutes to address a student's question, you can make the whole course positive and fulfilling for that student, and show the others your willingness to meet their agenda, not just your own.

Objectives. Objectives differ from goals because they are quantified and time-delineated. Although to appreciate art is a goal, to "be able to identify Van Gogh from Monet in three weeks" is an objective. For some classes, like a discussion of women's literature, goals may be much more important and evident than objectives. But for many other classes, from dance to job related skills, objectives are important to adult students who want to acquire a specific knowledge, and for whom the success of the class may depend on their ability to learn something they can use immediately.

End Results. Along with objectives for the course, you need to think of the end results. Where do you want your students to be at the end of the course compared with where they were at the beginning?

Before you start to think about the content of the course you should have three things clearly in mind and down on paper:

The course: A. Goals B. Objectives C. End Results.

Sample Course: Planting Strawberries

Goals:
1. *To convey an appreciation for the taste of natural, home-grown fresh strawberries;*
2. *To encourage local residents to plant more strawberries;*
3. *To start a 'Strawberry Club' for home growers interested in sharing knowledge and selling extra strawberries.*

Objectives:
1. *To compare the taste of homegrown natural strawberries with store-bought strawberries;*
2. *To demonstrate how to plant strawberries, including when, where, and how;*
3. *To show how to care for and pick strawberries;*
4. *To have each participant help in planting a number of strawberry plants.*

End Results:
   1. Students will know the difference in taste between store-bought and homegrown strawberries;
   2. Each participant will know how to plant strawberries at home.

Amount of Material

Having defined your goals, objectives, and end results, you then can estimate how much material to cover in the course. This is not always easy. Sometimes a class may get caught up in discussion and cover only a small fraction of what you had intended; other times the participants catch on sooner than you anticipated and you are racing through the material and run out of time. As a teacher you should be prepared for both outcomes, having enough material available, and yet being able to trim and cut back to the most essential points if the discussion or explanations take longer than planned. A long discussion on a particular point is a more positive sign of involvement and learning than is a silent audience. Covering many ideas may not be a sign of faster learning while questions, discussions, and disagreement over one single idea may mean more learning than quiet acceptance of a whole series of points.

There are various ways to arrange your material and different means to gauge how much to put in any one course. One way is to divide the material into three categories: material *essential* for the students to know; material *important* for the students to know; and material that is *nice* for the students to know.

Then you can make sure you convey what is essential, try to work in as much important material as possible, and add what is nice to know if you have time. With time running short, cut out the nice-to-know material and then the important items, and concentrate only on the essential points.

Slant or Approach

The goals for the class, particularly those of the learners, will determine the slant or approach you take with your subject. Every subject can be approached from many different directions and provide different end results and competencies. And the slant or approach may determine the success of the class. You could do a historical approach to car mechanics, or help people fix their own cars. You could talk about Italian cooking in general, or zero in on sauces as a subtopic. You could talk about modern novels, or relate them to the problem of interpersonal relationships and the change in family structure today. Here are eight ways you can slant the course.

1. *Basics.* A simple introductory course for people with little or no knowledge about the subject.
2. *Advanced.* New items people with a basic knowledge are unlikely to know.
3. *Subtopics.* Taking one particular area within the subject matter and concentrating or specializing on this.
4. *Demonstration.* Showing the class members how something is done or how something works.
5. *Practical, how-to.* Emphasizing the mechanics of the topic.
6. *They do it.* The participants actually learn by doing and come away with an ability they didn't have before.
7. *Current.* Focusing on the latest changes or trends in the subject area.
8. *Relating.* How the topic relates to some other topic, current event, or problem.

A course on bicycles could be slanted any number of ways, for example:

—an introduction to the workings of a bike (basic)
—a look at wind flow, BTU's and human energy in bike speed (advanced)
—cable brakes on a 10-speed bike (subtopic)
—see how bikes are made, a trip through a bike factory (demonstration)
—repairing your bike (they do it, how-to)
—vectors and the bike of the future (current)
—bicycles and urban pollution (relating).

By taking the wrong slant, a course can miss the mark and not meet participant expectations. On the other hand, an unsuccessful course can be turned into a successful one by taking a different slant. With so many different approaches to any given topic, one subject can be turned into many different courses, each one appealing to a different kind of learner.

After determining the slant and the amount of material you can cover in one course, the content can be organized to deliver it in the best way possible. Here are four ways in which content can be organized for delivery.

1. *Simple to complex.* Start with the easily understood, and move to the harder.
2. *General to specific.* Start with an overall scheme or theme, then get down to the specific items within that overall picture.
3. *Concrete to abstract.* Start with the here and now before moving to theories or concepts.
4. *Chronological sequence.* A historical sequence, starting at the beginning and working through history to today. Or any other time sequence.[1]

With your goals, objectives, end results, and material organized, you then can break the course down into each session or meeting.

Typical divisions for an individual class meeting include:

1. Introduction
2. Why the topic to be discussed is important
3. The central theme or concept
4. Elaborations on the theme or main point
5. Examples or demonstrations
6. Applications, conclusions or results
7. Summary of the main points
8. Questions and answers
9. A look ahead to the next class.

Educator Russ Robinson, in *Helping Adults Learn and Change*, offers the following points in helping to design an individual session.

For the beginning of the class, determine your lesson objective. Come up with a unit title. Then analyze and sequence the content needed, determining the key points. Relate today's topic to previous sessions and with the students' background. Outline the presentation of new content by listing important topics, selecting illustrations and examples, and choosing techniques or presentation. Decide on teaching devices and materials you will need. Develop a plan for application, or a student activity in applying the lesson. Prepare test questions, problems, or other evaluation tools. Summarize and review the lesson.[2]

Although selecting a unit title may seem artificial and too close to the stilted lesson plans developed for us as children, it illustrates a key point—that each class meeting is a separate entity.

Each class session is like a short story. It should have a beginning and an end. And the student should take something away from every class. When each session is a "neat unit," the student will remember more easily what was covered, tend not to confuse issues or topics, and be able to do or know something at the end of each class. The participant can then justify to himself or herself and to others why to return next time.

To do this, make up a worksheet for each class session. It does not have to be elaborate, nor long, but it will help you plan the session. Here is a simple outline for a class session.

Class	Session Number or Title		
Objective	*Content Outline*	*Techniques*	*Time*

In each class session you will be selling the whole course again because if the participant doesn't learn from each class, he or she may not be interested enough to return.

Unlike the school situation in which the students have to attend, you cannot afford to ramble too much, be too disorganized, or bore the participants. A little simple planning can help you avoid those mistakes.

After you have outlined the course goals and content, you can move from what you will say to ways you will say it. It is important to keep in mind four points in planning teaching techniques for your course.

1. Keep your presentations or talks short, 15 to 20 minutes at the most. If long explanations are necessary, the presentations should be broken up with practice sessions, questions, or other participatory interaction.

2. Involve the students as much as possible. Welcome questions, engage students in conversation, encourage discussion. Be sure to leave adequate time in your schedule for discussion.

3. Use a variety of techniques. Avoid gimmicks and fancy devices for their own sake, but integrate three to five different techniques or devices into each session. Each one breaks the monotony and keeps the group interested. Different techniques also help people learn in different ways. One person might learn from your presentation, while another from a slide show, a third from a drawing on a flip chart, and a fourth from the question-and-answer period.

4. Visual aids help the learning process. Flip charts, chalkboards, slides, overhead transparencies, models—all add to your presentation.

Facilities have a lot to do with the success of your interaction, and some planning should be done, if possible, to make your setting as conducive as possible to learning.

Materials Preparation

Your materials must be prepared as well. Too often handouts or reading materials are an afterthought, or sometimes no thought is given to them at all. Many an administrator has had the experience of the new teacher, enthusiastic and knowledgeable, who showed up with a reading list of ten books for a short, noncredit course, unaware that most working adults cannot and will not read so much material. The opposite extreme—no handouts, no references, no directions for further learning—is just as poor.

Although each class will vary in its needs for written materials, the following are general outlines for preparing materials.

1. Most adults won't have time to read a whole book, but chapters or articles are feasible. Following the copyright laws, using articles or chapters is a good way to convey information without burdening the student too much.

2. Other handouts can be prepared by you. This is the best way to convey most succinctly the information you deem most important. Be sure to use handouts well. Don't put down on paper things better said. Don't overdo handouts. Put down information participants should know or can use after the course. Use handout material for things it would take too long to copy in class, or take up too much valuable class time.

3. If possible, provide a reading list or list of references for further research or study. For practical classes, this might be a list of people, places, or other resources.

Overstructuring

Although there is no such thing as overpreparing for a class, there is the definite danger of "overstructuring" the course or an individual class. Overstructuring is simply cramming too many things into one time period, or controlling the class session so much that the participants lose all sense of participation, involvement, and enjoyment. It is definitely not wise to structure the class session so that one or more of the following mistakes occur.

—Every minute of the class session is scheduled.
—Too many facts, figures, and points are made within one time session, without adequate breathing time, reflection, or questions.
—There is inadequate time for discussion.

Preparation does not mean filling up the hour with things to say, or keeping participants running so fast with exercises, reports, and taking notes that they do not have time to absorb or interact. It takes forethought to schedule discussion, thought time, silence, or even a break when appropriate.

Preparing the Course. For Further Reading:
1. *Adults Teaching Adults*, by Verduin, Miller and Greer. Learning Concepts, Austin, Texas, 1977.
2. *Helping Others Learn*, by Patricia A. McLagan, Addison-Wesley Publishing Co., Reading, Massachusetts, 1978.
3. *Because They Want to Learn: A Handbook about Adult Learners for New Teachers of Adults*, Los Angeles City Schools, Los Angeles City Schools, Division of Career and Continuing Education, Los Angeles, 1977.

Chapter 5
Measuring Results

"Changingness, a reliance on process rather than upon static knowledge, is the only thing that makes any sense as a goal for education."
—Carl R. Rogers

In some learning situations it is either difficult or not particularly relevant for learners to assess and measure what they have gained from a course. In many learning situations, however, it is either important or necessary to measure the participants' progress. Credit courses, certificate programs, skill training, and basic education are all examples of classes that need to measure student learning.

Too few classes are adequately structured to measure a student's progress meaningfully.

When planning courses in which measuring student progress is important, Verduin, in *Adults Teaching Adults*, recommends these overall steps in planning the instruction activities:

A. Define terminal goals
B. Assess entering behavior
C. Define and organize the content
D. Select materials
E. Invent and/or select strategies
F. Create classroom climate
G. Assess learning[1]

Because the steps in measuring student progress differ from any other adult learning course only in the three areas of defining terminal goals, assessing behavior, and assessing learning, this chapter will concentrate on those three areas.

Defining Terminal Goals

Defining terminal goals for the learner should be stated in terms of behavioral objectives.

Try these suggestions in designing behavioral objectives:

a) Use the adult student as the subject of the behavioral objective. State specifically what the person is expected to do as a result of the learning.

b) Identify observable responses expected of the person and tasks to be performed.

c) Specify how the behavior is to be demonstrated so that learning can be observed.

d) Write the standards or quality of outcome desired.

e) Write your behavioral objectives in complete sentences.

From designing behavioral objectives or outcomes desired at the end of the course, you can move to writing instructional objectives or those objectives to be achieved during the class (as opposed to behavioral objectives, which are to be achieved after the course ends).

Instructional objectives should be brief enough to be remembered, clear enough to be written, and specific enough to be obtainable.[2]

Management specialist Robert Mager offers these hints on instructional objectives.

An instructional objective:

1. Says something about the learner.

2. Identifies an observable act, what the learner will be able to do.

3. Is about ends rather than means.

4. Describes conditions under which the learner will be performing the behavior.

5. Contains information about the level of performance that will be considered acceptable.[3]

Writing objectives for instructional plans is one of the more important instructional responsibilities of an adult educator. There are three ways to determine your instructional objectives. The first way is to observe and interview people performing the tasks being considered for inclusion in the course. What is the person doing? How does the person perform various tasks? Under what conditions and with what equipment does the person accomplish the task? How does the person perceive the task he or she is performing? What errors have been made? What needs to be improved? What would the person do differently?

The second way is to survey those tasks which professionals and organizations, like professional associations, recommend. The third way is for the teacher to use his or her own experiences to determine what should be taught.

Assessing Entering Behavior

Assessing entering behavior is probably the least recognized and performed step in conducting a course in which a change in behavior is to be measured. Assessing entering behavior is necessary to determine what the person has learned during the course. Testing at the end helps but certainly does not measure course achievement if entering behavior has not been measured.

Here are three ways to assess entering behavior.

1. Have the student attempt to perform the desired task or series of skill.
2. Measure the student's knowledge with a test.
3. More informally, ask each student how much he or she knows about the subject already. Or ask a set of general questions about previous experience or knowledge of the subject.

Assess Learning

Assessing an adult's learning properly can help him or her immensely. The assessment can provide an accurate picture of what the students know or can do, and can give them satisfaction in their achievements. It can direct their attention to areas where they are still weak or need improvement.

Unfortunately, much testing in adult education is vague, incomplete, and comes after the course is over—too late to help the learner. But there are good practices that, when followed, will yield positive assessment results. Those results will also be useful to you as the teacher in understanding how to improve your course.

How you measure your participants' learning depends on *What* you want to measure, *Where* you want to measure it, *Why* you want to measure it, and *When* you want to measure it.

What you can measure includes the cognitive domain, such as knowledge of facts, or understanding the meaning of something, which is done with a content test. The affective domain of values and attitudes is measured with an attitude survey, and psychomotor skills such as repairing a motor or playing tennis can be measured with a rating scale.

The content test is usually the easiest to administer because it evaluates one's knowledge of facts, questions, problems, and thoughts. The four standard ways of testing the cognitive domain are multiple choice, true or false, short answer, or essay questions. The first three are obviously easier to grade, but the essay test may provide more opportunity for learning and testing the depth of one's understanding, depending on the subject.

The attitude survey is the most difficult test to design because it measures the more diffuse and changing aspects of values and attitudes. It also subjects the student to discerning the "right" value or attitude rather than stating his "true" opinion.

Rating scales are good ways to measure skills. By constructing the proper steps and procedures, you can measure how well they are performed and give learners precise information about which activities they can achieve, and which ones still need work. Being able to achieve all of the required actions gives the learner a sense of satisfaction and achievement.

Knowledge or skill is measured either under natural or artificial conditions. Natural conditions refer to everyday life, on the job, at home, or in competitive situations. For example, the natural setting for using your skill in fixing a motor might be at work, and the natural setting for your tennis skills would be a tennis meet. Artificial conditions are the class setting.

Why you want to test your participants is an important consideration. If you want them to be ranked in relation to the other members in the class, you would use a norm-referenced test to find out who is best, good, average, fair, and poor. If you want your students to be measured by an objective standard you would use a criterion-referenced test. An essay exam in which one person earns an A, four receive Bs, ten get Cs, four get Ds, and one fails is an example of a norm-referenced test. On the other hand, a first aid class that tests the proper way to treat a stroke victim may pass everyone if all do the procedures correctly, or everyone may fail if no one can do the steps correctly.

Although norm-referenced examinations are common throughout our formal schooling, be sure that ranking in terms of others in the class is helpful before giving this kind of test. A graduating class in medical school illustrates the comparison between the two kinds of tests. You may have had someone tell you, "Did you know that 50 percent of the doctors today graduated in the bottom half of their class?" Although this is true each graduating doctor was also judged by some criterion tests to be fit to practice medicine.

When you want to measure the students is another consideration. Students' abilities should be measured when they enter the class so that gains from participating in your class can then be measured. Testing can be done either during the class or at the end of the class. The advantage of testing during the session is that students can then use the test to correct and improve themselves. Frequent testing can be used to determine the progress your students are making. When the results of the test are immediately made known to the students, you can also use a "post mortem" to review the subject and be a teaching tool.

To capsulize, your test should be composed of one element from each of the following.

What
   cognitive domain (content test)
   affective domain (attitude survey)
   psychomotor skills (rating scale)
Where
   natural conditions (everyday life, environment)
   artificial conditions (the class setting)
Why
   rank compared with others (norm-referenced)
   meets an objective standard (criterion-referenced)
When
   during the class (formative or in-progress evaluation)
   end of the class (summative evaluation)

Regardless of what kind of test you administer, it must be valid, reliable, objective, and practical.

Validity. The same answer given by two different people at two different times should be either correct or incorrect. It cannot be right for one respondent and wrong for another. The test answers should remain the same. In addition, the test should reflect what will happen in real life.

Reliability. The same test, given over a period of time, should yield consistent results. If a group of people take the test and all pass, and later take the same test and all fail, it would be an inconsistent and unreliable test.

Objectivity. The results should not be affected by the person administering the test.

Practicality. Given the constraints of time, cost, and convenience, the test should be practical enough to be given to a number of people over a period of time.

In preparing and marking the test, British educator H.R. Mills warns that the test should be comprehensive, covering various aspects of what was discussed in class, rather than concentrating on just one aspect.

"We all know the feeling of being unfairly treated when confronted by an examination paper that tests only a small fraction of what we have been working hard at, and encouraged to prepare," he says.[4]

He suggests preliminary tests should be a little harder than the final test to help stimulate the students to learn more. Although some instructors use tests to stimulate a lazy class, it is far more valuable to design tests to give confidence and encouragement to your learners. The best time to give a test is from several days to two weeks after the material was learned, enough time so that the material is assimilated before being tested. In grading your examinations, be careful not to change your standards as you go along, and take time out to rest if you are becoming tired because fatigue may affect your grading, Mills says.

Here are some guidelines, courtesy of Texas A&M University, for constructing and giving the four most common types of tests for content.

Guidelines for Constructing Tests

Multiple Choice Items

1. Each item should test one, and only one, central idea.
2. Each item should be independent of every other item. One item should not aid in answering another item.
3. Write as clearly, simply, briefly, and correctly as possible; eliminate all nonfunctional words.
4. Avoid textbook phraseology and examples; whenever feasible,

use new situations and terms.

5. The item stem should present the central problem and all qualifications; it should include all words that otherwise would occur in each alternative.
6. Avoid negatively stated items.
7. If an item includes controversial material, cite the authority whose opinion is being used.
8. Alternatives should be homogeneous in content, form, and grammatical structure.
9. There should be one, and only one, correct response; this alternative should be clearly correct.
10. All distractors should be plausible and attractive to students who do not know the correct answer; yet they should be clearly incorrect or inadequate.
11. Distractors may represent common misconceptions, logical alternatives, frequent mistakes, or other plausible but incorrect information.
12. Alternatives should not overlap, include, or be synonymous with each other.
13. Avoid irrelevant clues to the correct response provided by response length, grammar, repetition of key words, common associations, explicitness of response, etc.
14. If alternatives fall in a logical arrangement—e.g., alphabetically, by magnitude—list them in this order.
15. The position of the correct responses should not fall in a pattern but rather be randomized.

True-False Items
1. Items should deal with a single idea, not a combination of several ideas.
2. Express each item simply and clearly in words whose meanings are definite and precise; include no more than one qualifying phrase.
3. Statements should be entirely true or entirely false, not partially true and partially false.
4. The crucial element in the statement should be apparent to the student; the truth of the statement should not rest on trivial details or trick phrases.
5. Items should be based on significant facts, principles and generalizations.

6. Include approximately equal numbers of true and false items on the test; make sure correct responses do not fall in a pattern.
7. Whenever possible, use quantitative rather than qualitative terminology.
8. Do not create false statements by inserting "not" into true statements.
9. Avoid mere repetition of textbook statements and statements that are minor variations of textbook statements.
10. Avoid specific determiners—i.e., words like sometimes, never, always—that may provide clues to the correctness of the statement.
11. When items refer to controversial material or to matters of opinion or value, cite the authority whose opinion is being used.

Short-Answer Items
1. Try to phrase items so that there is only one possible correct response.
2. Phrase items so that the student is clear what type of response is demanded; that is, so he knows the length and preciseness of response required, or, in an item with a numerical response, the units in which the answer should be expressed.
3. The response, preferably, should be a single word or short phrase.
4. Avoid using statements taken directly from the text.
(Rules 5–7 apply to completion items.)
5. Omit only key words, not trivia.
6. Place the blank near the end of the sentence.
7. Avoid overmutilated items; include a maximum of two blanks within an item.

Essay Questions
1. The question should clearly and unambiguously define the task for the student, but without interfering with the measurement of the intended outcomes.
2. The question should indicate the direction and scope of answer desired.
3. The question should require the student to demonstrate his command of essential background knowledge.
4. Use questions that have clearly acceptable answers, rather than ones that only measure opinions or attitudes.

5. It is usually better to use more specific questions which can be answered briefly rather than fewer broad, general questions.
6. Do not use optional questions.
7. Start essay questions with phrases such as: compare and contrast, present the arguments for and against, give the reasons for, explain how (or why), give an example of, and similar phrases.[5]

Measuring Results. For Further Reading:
  1. *Teaching Adults*, by Gary Dickinson, General Publishing Company Limited, Don Mills, Ontario, 1973.
  2. *Developing Human Resources*, by Leonard Nadler, Gulf Publishing Company, Houston, 1970.
  3. *Choosing Evaluation Techniques*, by Hazel Taylor Spitze, Home Economics Education Association, Washington, D.C., 1979.

Chapter 6
The First Class

"And then you make them believe."   —Jerold Apps

The first class is important. In fact, it is not overstating to say it is critical to the success of your course. Your participants arrive, often as individuals who do not know each other. And they have some anxiety, some fear, of not knowing whether they will fit in, be able to master the subject, enjoy it, be humiliated, be frustrated, be bored, or whether the adult learning situation will be too hard for them.

And from that unrelated, anxious, skeptical number of individuals, you as the teacher have to put it all together—make them a group, get them to know one another, establish a relationship with them, excite them about the subject they will be learning, and encourage them to return for the next class.

As one participant remembers, "It was three times as scary." The participant recalled his first night in a cardio-pulmonary resuscitation (CPR) class with teacher Jim Frandy at the Lakeland Elementary School in Manitowish Waters, Wisconsin.

"It was scary because I didn't know any of the other students, and quite frankly, they were a little different from me. It was scary because the subject was death, and how I might, or worse, might not, save someone's life. And it was scary because the teacher was telling us we would have to take a test at the end of the course.

"But Mr. Frandy made everyone so at ease almost immediately. He was very reassuring. He told us who he was, asked us why we were there, and he told us to relax. That was easy because he was relaxed. He would pause, and then look at his notes, but then he would talk directly to us in a very informal manner. He gave us a little history of the Resuscitation Annies—those mechanical people we would be working on—and he added a touch of humor. I can't remember quite what he said, it wasn't a joke. And he made the test seem easy as well. He said, 'It is nothing to be scared of. It is supposed to find out what you know, not something to fail. We'll take it one step at a time, and whenever you can do it correctly, then you can take the test. The idea is for you to do it right.'

"He also told us something very important about himself, that he once had to use CPR, and although he did it correctly, the man died. I don't know why, but that made it less scary as well, to know something of him, and also to know that sometimes, even if you do it correctly, a person can still die."

Making that first class a success is a tall order, but one that can be achieved. And the satisfaction of having achieved a cohesive group interested in your subject after one meeting is worth the effort. And you will have help. Some of the participants will have taken courses before, and be much more at ease. Others will have had some contact or knowledge of the subject, and be willing to share their experience and excitement about the topic with the rest of the class. You also will have a class plan, and that scheme of introducing activities for the first class also will help you through.

The foremost adult educator in the country, Malcolm Knowles, tells about his own first class.

"The opening session, the opening hour or two or three in any activity is the single most critical time of the whole period in which I engage learners. It is at this time that we become acquainted with each other. It is during this time we survey the resources the students are bringing to the class. It is during this time we build a collaborative rather than a competitive relationship among the students in the group. We build an atmosphere of mutual trust, mutual respect, supportiveness, and I present myself as a human being. I also explain my role as facilitator and resource person, and what theoretical framework underlies the approach I use. I tell them I am a trout fisherman from Montana."[1]

Here's what should happen during the first class.

1. You should get to know the students, as many as is possible.
2. You should introduce yourself, and establish your "humanness."

3. The participants should be introduced to each other.
4. You should eliminate any fear or anxiety by providing a relaxing and informal activity.
5. Participants should be immediately invited to participate, most commonly by having them tell a little about themselves.
6. The subject should be introduced as well as what the course will cover.
7. The style of your teaching should be established and your techniques described to eliminate any fears of a boring class.
8. The participants should become involved in the course in some way.
9. You should encourage your participants' return by describing what they can expect next time.
10. You should try to get any preliminary feedback from your participants at the close of the class or afterward.
11. You should internally review the class session, what went well, what could have been done better, what you can do next time.

Preparing for the First Class

Although each class meeting needs preparation, your first class will differ from all of the other meetings. For that reason, you should design a special preparation worksheet just for the first class to accomplish all of the tasks, activities, and atmosphere-setting required for the first meeting.

Here is a sample worksheet covering all the aspects of the first class.

Activity	Method	Materials	Time
1. Welcome			
2. Introducing Myself			
3. Participants' Introductions			
4. Ice-Breaker			
5. Assessing Learner Needs (Why did you come?)			
6. Announcements			
7. Introduction of Subject/Topic			
8. Break			

   9. Participant Involvement
   10. Summary
   11. Personal Evaluation
      of First Session

The second step to your preparation is to go through each stage of the first session mentally and envision what will take place and how. This will give you a familiarity with the first class, so that when you actually do it, you will be more comfortable because you will have already "done it before" in your mind. It also will give you a chance to go through your "checklist" of activities, methods, materials and times to make sure everything is in order, and that you have not forgotten something needed for the class. For example, for a coffee break, do I have cups, sugar, coffeemaker, and so on?

The third step in your preparation is "rehearsing." By knowing your material well, you will establish confidence in your participants about you as an instructor. On the first meeting, you should "have it all together." This doesn't mean memorizing, and it certainly does not mean reading a speech or lacking spontaneity. But it does mean knowing your material fully and having everything in place—your notes, materials, instructional aids, and your thoughts—opening, topic in proper sequence, summary and closing.

Teachers, even those who have taught previous classes, are just as susceptible to a little nervous jitters as the participants, what Florence Nelson calls "First Nighter's Disease." To reduce some of that anxiety on your part, she recommends lots of rehearsing. In *Yes, You Can Teach*, she advises "In front of a mirror, on your way to work . . . practice. Then gather your family or friends and practice out loud. Don't memorize, but go through your main points over and over so that they become a part of your conversation."[2]

Step by Step

Let's go through that first class meeting, step by step.

1. Arrive early, well in advance of the class starting time, and before any participants are likely to arrive. Have the room or building "ready" by the time the students come. Make sure doors are unlocked, room directions clear, lights on. Adjust the chairs the way you want them, set up all the instructional equipment beforehand, get the refreshments ready—in short, be ready to roll. When the participants come in, they will feel welcome and the at-

mosphere will be set so you can spend time with them instead of threading the motion picture projector.

2. As each student arrives, welcome him or her at the door.

3. Spend some pre-class time with the participants. By now your notes should be in order, and you should not be reviewing your materials, but getting to know your students. If a few chairs still have to be rearranged, involve the participants in helping you. Break down some initial barriers and engage in small talk. Get to know, as best you can, some of the students. Find out if anyone has had previous experience with the topic, why they came, how they heard about the class, and so on. This pre-class chatter not only makes the participants more comfortable, but also may provide you with noteworthy examples to use when the class gets going.

4. Just before the class beings, do two things. Take a few deep breaths and relax. And two, make sure you are enjoying all this!

5. Welcome participants to class.

6. Introduce yourself. Participants are interested in knowing two things about an instructor. The first is that he or she is "qualified" to teach. Those qualifications are almost always viewed as experience or competence in the subject, not in terms of academic schooling or degrees obtained. If you have taught the course before say so. If you have experience in the subject matter describe it. If you have only a basic competence of the subject don't hide it. Be honest about it and your intent to teach only what you know.

Students want to know you are their "superior" in the subject about which they are to learn, but they also want to know that you are a peer in every other way. Distance, becoming an authority figure, or aloofness do not enhance adult learning. So you also want to establish a relationship with your participants that indicates some of your personal, though not necessarily private, characteristics. Adult educator Jerold Apps speaks of his own experience by noting that you try to make them relax, you tell jokes, refer to your own spouse or home or children to make them feel that you welcome personal experience in the classroom. "And then you make them believe," he says.[3]

7. The participants introduce themselves. It is important for the participants to know each other and to be involved in the class as soon as possible. Introductions are the first opportunity to involve each person in the class and that early involvement will help

keep the person interested throughout the class. Have all participants introduce themselves even if only one person doesn't know the rest. Even if everyone knows everyone else, it is often a good idea to do introductions, and have each person relay some new information to the rest of the group (My current fantasy vacation is . . .; One thing you don't know about me is that . . .), thus helping to make this group your group, a new experience, and possibly shaking up any pre-existing social patterns of interaction.

8. If your introductions have been short, and there is still a need to break down some of the barriers, to get participants further acquainted, or relaxed, or to introduce your subject matter in a unique way, an ice-breaker exercise often is used, and often welcome. There are numerous games or exercises to encourage people to interact with each other. Ice-breakers should not be contrived, artificial, pointless, or done "just because it is recommended." But they do help establish a learning climate, an atmosphere of trust and friendliness—and the feeling of security on the part of each adult learner is a vital prerequisite to that person's learning anything in your class. So it is worth the time getting to know one another and establishing a learning environment for the class.

9. Assess the needs of your learners. Each person in the class, of course, will have individual needs and wishes, and your one group session will not be able to meet every need of every student in the class. But you can make the class more meaningful and successful to them by trying to meet as many of their needs as possible. In assessing what your participants want out of your class, you may find that:

- A few expected something different from the class, and that you can, in these early stages, revise your course outline to meet their needs.
- Several individuals may want more emphasis or additional material in certain areas. Throughout the course you can spend some time meeting those individual wishes by devoting a few more minutes on a particular area or adding comments specifically because of a request.
- One or more individuals may be coming to the wrong class and they may wish to look elsewhere for the kind of learning they are seeking.

The advantage of finding out what your participants want to learn is twofold: you learn what they want and are more apt to provide the kind of learning that will satisfy the most learners; and they understand more clearly why they are in the class, and are better able to benefit and evaluate their own experience based upon a clearer idea of what they expected.

Many teachers "assess learner needs" by simply going around the class and asking participants to express why they came and what they hope to learn. Another way to do it is to play a game or do an exercise which will bring out the students' expectations. A more formal way is to have each person fill out a survey asking more specific questions about what they would like to see take place in the class. Another way is to hand out your course outline, show what you plan to do for the entire session, and actively seek participant response as to whether this meets their needs.

And finally, some teachers introduce the subject and then at the end of the first class meeting ask for student responses and changes in the course outline. Seeking to involve the learners in suggesting areas to emphasize rarely leads to a total revision of the course although that occasionally happens. But it is always good to be open to that kind of dramatic change. More often it helps the teacher to expand upon some topics and limit others not so important. The result is usually more satisfied learners, a happier teacher, and more learning taking place.

10. Make any announcements and get any housekeeping tasks out of the way before you get into the subject of the course. If you need to register students, do so. If you need a form filled out, do it now. If you need to tell them where the restrooms are, or the coffeepot, combine your "important trivia" and dispense with it then.

11. Introduce your subject. This may mean going over your course outline. It may mean "getting your feet wet" in the topic area but saving the full plunge for the second class. Or it may mean jumping right in and taking off. It is important, however, that the students leave with some new piece of information or knowledge after the first session and every session. Each session must be an achievement, an accomplishment no matter how small, in the learner's mind because for adults every hour must be justified and meaningful. It is too easy for adults not to return. They get tired, there are distractions, there are obligations, there are unforeseen circumstances, and thus each class session, and certainly the first one, must be a rewarding one. It is this time during the class that the instructor will want to not only introduce the

subject matter, but also introduce the style of teaching to be used as well. You need to sell your students not just on the subject matter but on your teaching as well. So use different techniques, involve the students as much as possible, and make the presentation interesting, lively, and diverse.

12. If your class lasts more than an hour, be sure to plan a break. Breaks are not just wasted time. They are important for adults to recoup their energy and attention, to recap a little of what they have learned, and to know the other participants better. Often a couple of students will spend the time discussing with you or other students some aspects of what has been covered, exploring it further. Having refreshments available is always appreciated, and sometimes teachers will have structured breaks. But most often it is best to let your students alone and allow them to mingle if they wish or to go outside. As a teacher you can also use the break effectively. You can review notes and prepare for the next phase of the class meeting. You can get to know your students better, and gather more information which can be used in class as examples of invitations to involvement. And you can just observe the dynamics of the group's interaction. Although a break may be just a break for the students, it is often an excellent opportunity for the teacher to learn about the students.

13. At the end of the first class you will want to summarize what they have learned, to point out, possibly in a subtle way, what they have achieved, and in this way give them something to take back home. You also need to get them excited about returning and stimulate their interest further in the course. As Florence Nelson says, "A simple goodbye is not enough. Give your students something to look forward to."[4] So tantalize them with next week's agenda or activity.

14. Be available for five to twenty minutes of informal contact with the participants after the end of the class meeting. This will provide some individual attention, maybe answer a question someone might have been too embarrassed or hesitant to ask in front of the whole group, or pursue some area further with a curious student. But before the class, during the class, or afterward, British educator Ralph Ruddock warns, "Beware of being captured by a pub-group, sub-group, or tea-group. That demotes other members."[5] Being overly familiar or attentive to any one person or section of the class can be discouraging to others.

15. Immediately after the class is over, take a few moments to reflect on the class and relive it one more time. What went well? What didn't go well? What could be improved for next time? What should be changed for next time?

Some of these steps are obvious, some of them just common sense. Ralph Ruddock says, "Some of it is so general as to fall within the category of good manners, a very minor category in school teaching, but significant in adult teaching as an expression of regard between tutor and class member."[6]

The first session is critical for the success of your course. It is a tough task to accomplish all of the things that need to be done in that first hour or so. But having done it, you should be able to look back on it, and not only say you survived the first class, but also that it was a good experience as well.

The First Class. For Further Reading:
1. *Yes, You Can Teach*, by Florence Nelson, Carma Press, St. Paul, 1977, 59 pages.

Chapter 7
Involving Your Participants

"To know how to suggest is the art of teaching."
—Amiel

The most dynamic and variable element in your adult learning situation will be the participants themselves. Working with this resource is both a challenge and an opportunity to make your class exciting. You can unearth potential, ideas, and interaction you and they probably did not know exist.

Expectations are central to tapping your human resources. It is important for you to know who your participants are, what they expect from the class, why some of them may drop out, what they can and want to contribute, and how to adjust to their differing expectations.

Finding Out Who Your Participants Are

As soon as you can, find out who your participants are. Ask the institution sponsoring your course who usually registers. Before the first class, talk to as many participants as possible. During the first class, you may want to spend a little time discussing past experience and hobbies. After class or between classes it is valuable to continue learning about the participants.

That diversity is one of the greater assets your course can have, but to use it properly, you have to know it exists. Knowing *who* your participants are is essential.

Meeting Participant Expectations

Find out what your participants expect from your class. The success of the class depends upon meeting their needs. Although you as the teacher may feel their hopes are obvious—learning the subject you are offering—that may not be the whole story.

By being flexible enough to meet different intentions, you can improve the class. That may mean taking a break in the middle of the class to serve refreshments, encouraging people to meet afterward at Joe's Bar, or spending a session talking about job opportunities in your field of study. By adjusting your agenda slightly to meet those wishes, you will find a more enthusiastic group of individuals in your class.

Here are some questions to ask your participants individually or in a group. The answers will serve as tip-offs to what they anticipate, and also what they might contribute to the group.

—Have you studied this topic before?
—Why did you decide to take this course?
—Have you had any experience or work in this area before?
—What would you like to do with this course after you are finished?
—What is your work?
—What would you like to be doing in two years?
—How did you hear about this course?

Students as Participants

Probably the greatest resource for your class and your teaching will be the participants themselves. Unlike a formal educational classroom where students are not perceived to have much knowledge in the subject, you will find your participants have skills, talents, and perspectives you can and should use in the course.

Your learning situation will differ from a traditional classroom. There will be many kinds of people with different backgrounds. That variety can be turned into an exciting learning process by playing on the worldliness of the people in the group. Every person in the group has had some life adventures, and just as important, relates to what you are discussing from his or her own perspective. By using the group members' own experiences, the teacher can involve them in the learning process to a much greater

degree than if the teacher only used his or her own situation or merely asked for the members' opinions.

Tapping the knowledge of your participants has at least three benefits. First, their learning is enhanced by being involved. Second, their feedback and interaction can substantiate your input and be a good teaching aid for your points. And third, they will come up with some facts, information, or ideas you hadn't considered.

Do not make the mistake of being apprehensive about your participants' knowledge. Too many teachers are defensive or condescending about their students' comprehension. They try to avoid student input, seek to establish their superior wisdom, or try to correct students needlessly. These reactions may come from a false impression about what the teacher is and is supposed to do. You are not supposed to know everything about the subject; and the students are not presumed to understand little or nothing about the subject. You can learn as much as the students, and you can learn *from* the students. The students do not expect you to possess complete wisdom. Your participants' impressions, whether correct or whether totally misinformed, are important to them, and just as critical to you the teacher if you are to help them learn 'the true way' and obtain more enlightened information or skills.

Students respect a teacher more for admitting less than Zeus-like competence in the subject area. They know no one has a monopoly on any subject.

Teachers must deal with two general kinds of training students bring to class. The first is genuine information and skills, and you should recognize, praise, and use that talent in your class. The second is misinformation resulting from inadequate or less than satisfactory previous learning. Instead of attacking that inadequate information, the teacher can point to the one or two correct statements the student is making and elaborate on them, or use the student in examples demonstrating your information.

A teacher may even find someone in the class more knowledgeable than he or she. One science fiction enthusiast, who had studied and read and written science fiction for years, offered a class on the topic. When the class met, the teacher was surprised to find out that everyone not only had a good deal of knowledge in science fiction, but also had published a work of science fiction . . . everyone, that is, except the teacher. Instead of giving up or being resentful, he used their experience and they used his, and each learned from the other.

Here are ways to tap your participants' skills and knowledge.

1. Encourage questions and comments from your participants.
2. Ask your students for experiences relating to the topic you are discussing.
3. Ask your students to bring to class examples pertaining to the subject.
4. Divide into subgroups for discussion or learning from each other. Sometimes a group leader facilitates the group's productivity.
5. Divide into pairs and have the students share an experience with each other. Sometimes those experiences can be relayed to the entire group, but this is not always necessary or time-efficient.
6. Ask an individual to take 10 minutes and relate a particular experience about the topic.
7. Take turns having participants give presentations or demonstrations to the entire class.

In addition to participation being a good process technique, the learning will be increased by using the students as participants. The more they are involved in a group, the better people learn. People will also learn by listening to and interacting with other group members. The teacher often learns from the participants who may offer different views on the subject. If the teacher spends less time in solo performances and the participants are involved in the group, people will be attentive and the learning will be enhanced.

The Teachable Moment

One of the more elusive, rarely discussed, and exhilarating experiences is "the teachable moment." It is one of the more difficult situations for the teacher to handle, mainly as it comes without warning and because it requires the teacher to relinquish control of the class. The sociologist Havighurst first defined the "teachable moment" in 1947 as a time in one's life when one is ready to learn, eager, and able to absorb what the teacher has to offer. It can be a time in life, but it can also be a time during the class session when students suddenly perk up.

Many teachers have had the experience. One is teaching, and

the students have typical expressions on their faces—a few are interested as always, while others look bored, or stare off, or try to interject their own ideas. And then someone says something and a mental bell rings, eyes light up, heads turn, ears tune in, and the entire class is suddenly alive. It is an exhilarating time that may last for seconds or minutes, yet a time when a word or gesture from you as the teacher may mean more than the rest of the hour, or sometimes the whole course. It is a moment that has been defined and shaped not by the teacher, but by the participants. They have caught onto something, and whether it is a comment from the teacher, or just as likely, a comment from another participant, the learners have defined their interest and made this learning moment theirs. The "teachable moment" is really a peak learning moment because now is not the time to lecture or talk, but to respond to the participants. It is the time to try to enhance and extend that peak learning moment.

For the teacher, it is a difficult time. You have been proceeding with your agenda, constructing an orderly pattern of ideas and points, and abruptly this diversion occurs. Often the learning moment centers not on an idea you have just stated, but a statement or even totally different idea from a participant. Often the catalyst for the learning moment takes the discussion far afield, off the central thesis you are building, maybe even off the subject of the course.

Your first response as a teacher is to try to regain control. You may try to limit discussion because time is running out, and move on to your next point. The class, after all, has cut you off in the middle of your series of points. Or you may try to use their enthusiasm to re-establish their interest as you pursue your next topic. Or you may try to interject and use the moment to convey your most important ideas. But all those responses usually just inhibit or cut short the learning moment.

The learning moment is the learner's moment, and the best help the teacher can provide is to let go, allowing the learners to set the agenda and direct the conversation. Your most valuable contribution is simply to have created the environment. You can and should participate in the learning moment, but as a learner, an equal, not dominating or controlling it. If you can recognize that magical moment, let it happen, and flow with it, you will participate in one of the more rewarding experiences of being a teacher, "the teachable moment."

Dropouts

Every teacher should expect people to drop out of class. Sometimes only a few people will leave and sometimes half the class will disappear, but you can count on somebody dropping out. Whether this has a debilitating effect or is expected often means the difference between whether the class is perceived as a failure.

One factor contributing to the dropout rate is the fact that the criteria for a voluntary class are so much higher than for a more traditional school class. For some reason, both the teacher and the participants expect a great deal more from the class than they would expect from a comparable more formal class at a university. The participants want their time to be used wisely and are sensitive to class sessions of low quality. The teacher is also conscious of making the time together a learning one. Because it is so easy for participants to walk out or just not show up the next time, each class has to be rewarding to attract the participants next time. Because there are no outside inducements, such as credits or possibly high cost, the adult class has fewer holds on the participants than does a traditional class.

Be this as it may, there will always be people dropping out of your class. Some people will discover they know much of what is being discussed. Others will find the topic is not quite what they had expected. Still others will sit in on a few classes and learn all they want to about the subject. A few may have to leave because of extenuating circumstances such as illness, work responsibilities, or family. These are legitimate reasons and ought to be considered so. People should feel free to direct their own course of learning and not be boxed in by a class situation.

Other less legitimate reasons for dropping out of a class include lack of interest and lack of self-discipline. These, of course, are not under the control of the teacher and are hard to combat. A few words at the beginning of the course about responsibility to the group might be helpful. Beyond briefly mentioning this, the teacher can do little to keep people in the group in addition to preparing for each session and facilitating the group well.

Not all of this motion is negative. Some teachers have experienced a "reverse dropout," in which people come back later, additional people come to the class, or participants drop out and show up again when the class is offered in the next session. And it is not unusual to have participants bring along a friend or two to a particularly intriguing class.[1]

Whether one person drops out or half the group leaves, the teacher should not let this hinder the class in any way. If you expect some people to drop out and don't attribute this to your own abilities as a teacher, you can concentrate on those who remain in the group.

Adjusting to Differing Expectations

Sometimes the expectations of one or more students will differ from yours. This is a difficult situation but one that cannot be ignored. The best way to deal with differing expectations is to get them out front and clearly defined. What do you want? What do I want? What is going on now? And how can we work it out to our mutual satisfaction? If it is an individual or two, you can talk to them and work out something that does not redirect the entire class. You could spend part of a class addressing their special interests. You could spend time after the class on their particular needs or interests. Or you could suggest resources for them to explore their interest independently. If more than just a few have differing expectations you should re-evaluate the course. Perhaps you can change the course, perhaps they can be enthusiastic about your direction for the class, or perhaps you can design another class for later.

Part of the joy of teaching adults is interacting with and exploring the skills, talents, and ideas of your participants. Although the diverse perspectives and unexpected feedback may occasionally challenge your facilitating abilities, the overall outcome is a creative and productive interaction that is rewarding to participants and teacher alike.

Involving Your Participants. For Further Reading:
  1. *Learning How to Learn*, by Robert M. Smith, Follett Publishers, Chicago, 1982.

Chapter 8
Teaching Techniques

"Not all learning comes from books. You have to live a lot."
                                                    —Loretta Lynn

Throughout this book we have stressed flexibility in teaching techniques, and this chapter will provide you with ideas on ways to achieve that variety in your teaching. The next few pages will be devoted to ways to lead a discussion, how to ask a good question, making a presentation, ways to arrange people, ice-breakers, devices and aids, out-of-class ideas, and exercises for small groups. Taken together, they represent a smorgasbord of tips and pointers from which you can choose.

There is no best technique to use in teaching adults, and the only bad technique is the one that is used repeatedly with the same group. Try several new ideas every time you teach; as in everything else, some of them will not work while others will be a surprising success. The variety and experimentation will also keep you interested in each class.

These suggestions are like ingredients for a stew. Mix them as you wish, and be sure to add your own special flavoring to the pot to make it unique to you.

Modes of Teaching

For the informal adult-oriented teaching you will be doing, there are basically four types of learning formats, depending on what kind of subject you are teaching. Each one is designed to gain maximum involvement from the participants and be as attractive a process as possible. You should choose your format and then elaborate upon it, using some techniques to enhance the model. Sometimes it is possible to use two or more modalities for one class, but usually the modality is restricted by your choice of subject.

Group Discussion. The group discussion has replaced the formal classroom procedure as the most common format for adult learning. It is generally used for idea related topics, including current events, philosophy, personal growth, as well as academic subjects involving reading and discussion.

To prevent the situation from dissolving into a bull session, the teacher should introduce new subject material each meeting in an informal talk. Uninterrupted lecturing or one-way communicative styles should be avoided at all times. The group discussion is usually located in an informal environment, such as a living room, with people seated so that they are able to see and respond to others. If the people introduce themselves at the beginning of the class, they will feel more open about contributing remarks and comments.

In the group discussion format, the teacher needs to develop creative ways of introducing material to the group and has to be attentive to involving the members in discussion. A knowledge of group process, facilitating, and group dynamics helps this format. The creative use of reading materials is problematic. Books and articles contribute greatly to the learning situation, yet reading assignments are often burdening to people who have little extra time for reading. Assigning one or two articles or a chapter of a book is one solution.

Over-the-Shoulder Demonstration. The over-the-shoulder demonstration format is most often used with practical skills classes, such as small appliance repair, carpentry, and auto mechanics. The attractiveness of this format is that it brings into the learning situation the material about which the group is talking.

The location of the class should be in a room free of furniture that might be in the way. A church basement or meeting room is appropriate. The teacher starts by talking about a particular aspect of the topic, and then moves quickly from talking to doing, for example, fixing a lamp while the class looks on. It is important that people be as close as possible to the action, so they can ask questions and discuss what is happening while the teacher is demonstrating. Then, depending on the resources available, the teacher can guide the participants as they perform the activity just demonstrated.

Sometimes a "chalk talk" on the chalkboard or using an easel for making a point enables the teacher to add theoretical points or ideas to the demonstration. Though seemingly simple, it is important with this model (as with the others) to plan objectives for each session. The format stays away from book learning and concentrates on the tangible, the concrete, thus making it a captivating format.

Show-and-Do Involvement. Unlike the others, the show-and-do format revolves around the participants rather than the teacher. It is most often used in arts and crafts kinds of classes where each participant is to create or build something individually. Examples of the format are painting, drawing, chess, and weaving.

The method is the most involving, with each participant doing or learning while the teacher demonstrates. The teacher injects new ideas or suggestions by interrupting the group and introducing a new idea at once.

A variation on this is to take the group out of the classroom and into the setting where the activity takes place, such as using a lake for sailing instruction or a garage for auto mechanics.

Formal Classroom Instruction. At times a formal classroom setting is most appropriate for learning. Generally, the formal setting—a room geared for learning rather than relaxing, desks or chairs arranged to give the teacher maximum attention and authority, and a rather traditional approach to instruction—is inappropriate for adults who do not want credits or job skills. But for those situations, and others, a classroom setting may get results. Basic education classes such as writing and mathematics or job skills classes such as typing or shorthand are examples. Traditional approaches, individualized instruction, and other methods can be explored here.

One final format should be mentioned, and that is the project format. Projects are simply learning and doing situations in which the class works to produce something while they are learning. The advantages of this style of learning are twofold: 1) the group learns by doing, an acknowledged learning method, and 2) the people in the group gain a sense of accomplishment. Examples of classes in which the project method would be useful are dome building and community power structures. The first class would actually build a dome while the second group would research their town and write a report on their community's power structure.

Leading A Discussion

If there is any teaching method to be favored over all the others, it is probably the group discussion. The group discussion lends itself particularly well to adults. It can be used in most any type of class and can be adapted to any teaching format, whether you are using the discussion, demonstration, how-to, or formal classroom mode of teaching.

Discussion is a good teaching method for several reasons. It is good for setting the climate, and fostering warmth, rapport, and interest among people in the group.[1] It produces interaction among learners, and motivates them to inquire further into the subject. It is also a form of feedback on their progress and serves as a nonthreatening way for adults to test their knowledge.

Confining a good discussion to just one hour is difficult. The optimal length is from one to two hours, with a break if needed. More than two hours is probably too much, less than an hour is probably too little for a discussion to reach fruition. If you have less than one hour, you can still conduct a discussion, but it will need to be more directed, involve you more as the initiator, and less should be expected from the abbreviated discussion.

Here are some suggestions in designing and facilitating a discussion.

—Arrange the group in a circle.

—Have everyone, including yourself, seated.

—Don't make any speeches.

—Allow 15 minutes for the discussion to get under way.

—Set a clearly defined question before the group. Sometimes it helps if the initial question is set in personal terms. For example, don't ask what conservatism is. Ask "Are you a conservative?"

—Keep the discussion on track. Try to limit your participation to areas that are important or overlooked, but assume responsibility for the direction of the discussion.

—Take time every once in a while to draw loose ends together.

—Give a sense of progress or satisfaction with the discussion, add a shape or contour to it so participants can see what they have achieved, and end on a positive note.

—Close the discussion with a summary and compliments to the participants for a job well done.

Perhaps the most difficult job in facilitating a discussion is dealing with the vocal ones at both ends of the scale—the loud, talkative, or disruptive individuals, and the quiet, inhibited, and passive folks. The approach to each type differs.

Those who have had too much to say and are preventing others from participating should be dealt with firmly and frankly. You should be polite, with the courtesy probably diminishing if your friendly suggestions are not heeded.

Here are some phrases to use.

"Frank, we've appreciated your comments. Now let's hear what the others have to say."

"Shirley, why don't we give Pat, Anne, and some of the others a chance to say something?"

For a discussion to succeed no one person should dominate it, and whatever measures are necessary to accomplish that objective should be used, including asking the disruptive person to leave if all else fails.

Quite another tack needs to be used to bring out someone who is quiet, shy, reserved, or not used to talking in a group. Here you need to be subtle and delicate in your efforts. Many of the best discussion leaders adhere to one of the "bill of rights" in discussions—the right to remain silent. Pestering or annoying people into talking will not achieve their or the group's goals, and some people truly prefer to be silent. But many others are simply inhibited and appreciate being drawn into the discussion.

You can tell after one or two overtures which persons are responding and which ones are not.

Here are some techniques to bring people into the discussion.

—Don't single out an individual as the quiet one, or make a point of turning the group's attention to the individual. Instead, ask a number of people for their opinion, including the person you are trying to bring out.

—Turn to the quiet person for a response.

—Try to involve the quiet person at first in a "starter" question, like a response, yes or no answer, or personal opinion, rather than asking a difficult or risk-taking question for openers. Some examples: "Brenda, what do you think of what Kent just said?" "Andrew, would you agree or disagree with that?" "Paul, do you personally think media news is slanted these days?"

—Give a light quick compliment to the person you are trying to bring out after a response. "Thank you," "Good," "Interesting point," are all nonelaborate yet encouraging words.

Not every discussion is perfect. Not every group will come up with an astonishing new theory or invention worth patenting. But discussions do work. Their effect is both immediate and long-term. You probably won't be aware of all the benefits taking place. Yet the time and energy you put into leading a discussion will doubtless pay off, in part because a good discussion is the epitome of what learning is all about—sharing.

Making Presentations

The essence of a good class presentation is not what you say but how you say it. This is not to detract from the content of what you have to offer. It is simply a recognition that adults will remember more, and learn more, if you say what you have to say clearly and methodically.

A magazine once conducted a survey on how much students remembered from a psychology class. First they had a psychology professor teach a class, and then an actor who had little or no knowledge of psychology. The students remembered more of what the actor said than what the professor said. Fortunately, you don't have to be an actor to make a good presentation, but some of the techniques are similar—like timing, a good opening and closing, and knowing when to stop.

The first thing to remember in making a presentation is not to think of it as a lecture. The lecture, even a good lecture, with its podium, lifeless notes, lack of interaction, concentration on subject matter regardless of the type or size of audience, is not a model for designing a presentation for adults. Instead think in terms of discourse, talking, or conversation. A conversation is fresh every time, has plenty of interaction, concentrates on the listener as much as the content of what is being said, and is a much better model for constructing a presentation. Some may immediately associate conversations with rambling, talking too long, changing the subject, and being disorganized. But these are poor conversational practices that also make presentations ineffective.

The second most important thing about presentations is that they are rarely too short, and often too long. Talking too long is probably the most common error in making presentations, and can damage an otherwise excellent presentation. Keeping an imperfect presentation short can improve it in the minds of your listeners.

As one elderly Muppet told the other one from their balcony seats, "I like that last number."

"Oh, what did you like about it?"

"It was the last number."

So too are adults appreciative of talks that end on time. It is better to leave your audience hungry for more than to leave them wishing there was less.

The three aspects to be concerned about in making a good presentation are content, preparation, and delivery.

In thinking about the content of your presentation, determine what is relevant and important and concentrate on that. Try to reduce or eliminate any other points which may be irrelevant, confusing, not important to know, or might even contradict what you are trying to convey. Adult educator Florence Nelson notes that irrelevant words, sentences or ideas confuse the learner, and she also shakes her head at comments that are not even on the topic at all. "What Aunt Sara said at dinner last night is of no consequence if it does not apply to the subject," she reminds us.[2]

The content needs to be geared to your audience's degree of familiarity. Your presentation should not be over their heads, nor should it be condescendingly basic if your listeners are already past that point. Determine as best you can the level of comprehension your audience will have.

Preparing your presentation should be similar to preparing for each class session. There should be three parts to your presentation: 1) the introduction, in which you outline what you will talk about; 2) the main body of the presentation; and 3) the ending, including a summary covering the most important aspects of your talk. It is not a poor practice to repeat the most significant points. In fact, it is a better practice if you can say the same thing differently each time.

When one backwoods orator was asked why his speeches were so good he replied, "Well, first I tells em what A'hm goin ta tell em; then I's tells em; and then Ah tells em what I tole em."

A lack of preparation in making presentations is bad, and too much preparation is just as bad, because it may lead to too much information in too short a time period. Don't try to teach too much in one session. Do one or two ideas or skills well, and be pleased with that.

The most important aspect about delivery is to speak to your participants. As Florence Nelson warns, "You are not teaching skills or knowledge. You are teaching people. You must speak their language."[3] In speaking their language you should be precise and economical in your words, speak clearly, and project your voice. Try to reduce the number of "uhs" and "ers" you use, as well as any pet words or phrases that might become repetitious. The rest is pacing and timing, delicate and critical aspects of speaking best learned through practice.

Kenneth Eble, in his book, *The Craft of Teaching*, has these Do's and Don'ts about making a good presentation.

Don't
—begin without an introduction
—have a lack of contact with the audience
—remain in a fixed posture, with your attention on your notes
—use a monotonous voice
—display false modesty
—use repeated hesitations
—get into private quarrels with other authorities.

Do
—fit the material into the time allotted
—seek precise examples and illustrations
—stimulate the audience's interest
—improvise
—provide for "breathing spaces" and time for questions
—provide an ending every time, but maintain a continuity with what lies ahead
—develop a range in voice, gestures and physical movement. Root out mannerisms and affectations
—listen to yourself
—be guided by the audience.[4]

One way to improve your delivery is to ask a close friend, spouse, or class member you know well and trust to sit in on the presentation and critique it. Ask him or her to pay particular attention to a mannerism you are trying to eliminate or some other habit. Talk to your friend afterward and make sure he or she makes some critical observations and doesn't just try to reassure you or make you feel good.

How to Ask a Good Question

One of the more potent weapons in your teaching arsenal is the good question. With it, you can keep the group together, share values and ideas, and explore new horizons of possibilities. The good question can make your class exciting while the poor question can provoke boredom.

Many proper and beneficial uses for asking a question include:
—As a lubricant to keep the group together and interested;
—To argue or set up poles or opposites;
—To share existing attitudes, values, or ideas class members hold;
—To get participants to say things you would say, but have greater effect when said by a participant;
—To explore deeper and come up with new ideas or understanding.

There are also poor uses of a question. Don't use a question to:
—Reprimand someone or test one's ignorance;
—Select or call attention to the better students;
—Fill time;
—Reach a foregone conclusion or lead people along a predetermined path;
—Put people on the spot; or when there is always a right and wrong answer to each of your questions.

There are generally three types of questions. One is the question asking for facts or known information. "When did James Joyce write *Ulysses*?" is an example. These questions are good to open a discussion or presentation, to capture or rekindle the class's attention, to promote active listening, and of course, as recall or test questions. Some ways of phrasing the question include using some of these words, who, where, what, when, why, how, state, name, identify, list, describe, relate, tell, recall, give, and locate.

There are questions of interpretation or evaluation. These questions ask people to compare, contrast, set a value on a certain item, or put something into perspective. They are useful in fostering critical thinking, and they also are good discussion questions. "Which alternative sources of energy show the most promise today?" is an example.

Some ways to phrase an evaluative question include using one of these words: evaluate, analyze, judge, compare, contrast, differentiate, calculate, measure, appraise, deliberate, and estimate.

A third kind of question asks the participants to think deeper and come up with a creative answer usually not previously discussed. These questions urge people to think beyond what was known or talked about. "What would you do if you could run the economy?" is one such question. Creative questions can start with any of these words: make, create, speculate, design, invent, construct, devise, predict, develop, what would have happened, and what would you have done.

Here are some tips on asking a good question.

• Ask questions that have few wrong answers, and try to follow up incorrect answers with other questions that lead the class in the right direction without highlighting an incorrect statement.

• Follow up an answer with another question to the same person, or by asking the same question to another person, or by asking the follow-up question to another person. This generates ideas and builds the discussion level.

• To bring out different points of view or clarify missed points, ask a "devil's advocate" question that might not correlate to your own position but sheds more light on the topic.

• Diffuse the discussion among all the class members by asking a reaction question to those not involved in the discussion. "Maria, how do you feel about what Burt just said?" is one example.

• Silence after a question is not necessarily bad. Allow some silence before trying another question or answering your own question to encourage thinking and participant responsibility for the discussion.

• Sometimes deliberately throwing questions to people on different sides of the room, or even going around the group with your questions helps build the level of involvement.

• If your participants start directing their answers and then their questions to each other, that can generate excellent participation and ideas.

You do not have to be the starting and ending point for each comment. You can encourage others to address each other with a nod or faint expression indicating it is acceptable to address one another, such as "Go ahead."

• Good questions to start a discussion are those asking for people's existing ideas, such as whether they agree or disagree about a particular issue. After letting them state their present values or attitudes, you can then go on to more tough questions involving creative thinking or postulating.

When used in a class discussion, your questions should seek to stimulate discussion and involve as many people as possible. The discussion should grow like a spiral, involving more people and rising to greater heights of ideas and thinking as you go. To help do that, think of questions that will fit together in a sequence or culminate in generating new ideas. As Kenneth Eble says, "Try to achieve a rhythm in a series of questions so the group arrives at moments of larger understanding."[5]

Arranging People

How you arrange the class often can determine the kind and extent of interaction you will have. Think carefully about how the seating arrangement will affect the discussion. For example, the more people can see each other, the more they will be involved in discussion. Thus, circles and U-shaped designs promote discussion. For more formal presentations where you want to be the center of attention and want questions rather than discussion, perhaps the classroom style or theater style of seating is more appropriate.

Also consider redesigning the room arrangements during class when the group wants to break for discussion. This variation in seating will stimulate a different kind of activity.

Russell Robinson, in *Helping Adults Learn and Change*, offers 10 standard types of room arrangements: theater style, herringbone style, U-shaped, diamond, hexagon, conference, circle, classroom style, small semi-circles, and banquet style.[6]

For more informal classes, a "living room style" with people seated randomly might encourage a relaxed atmosphere for discussion.

Ice Breakers

Ice breakers are techniques used at the beginning of the first class to reduce tension and anxiety, to acquaint participants with

71

each other, to immediately involve the class in the course, and to acquaint the teacher with the class members.

Use one or more as you see fit. Don't be afraid to experiment and try a different approach, but use an ice breaker because you want to not as a time-filler or because an outline says it should be used. Be creative and design your own variations.

Here are ten types of ice breakers and some variations.

Introduce myself. Participants introduce themselves and tell why they are there. Variations: Participants tell where they first heard about the class, how they became interested in the subject, their occupation, hometown, favorite television program, or the best book they have read in the last year.

Introduce another. Divide the class into pairs. Each person talks about himself or herself to the other, sometimes with specific instructions to share a certain piece of information. For example, "The one thing I fear most is . . ." or "One thing I am particularly proud of is . . ." After five minutes, the participants introduce the other person to the rest of the class. Variations: Have each person write something on a blank index card, pass out the cards, and have people find each other first before making the introductions.

Character descriptions. Have people write down one or two adjectives describing themselves. Put these on a stick-on badge. Have class members find someone with similar or opposite adjectives and talk for five minutes with the other person. Variations: Have each person think up an adjective describing himself, for example, Hopeful Sue; have an adjective start with the same letter as the name, such as, Roaming Robert; relate favorite food, wine, color, famous person; if I were a food, I would be a _____; if I were an affliction, I would be a _____, because _____.

Find someone. Each person writes on a blank index card one to three statements, such as favorite color, interests, hobby, vacation. Pass out the cards so everyone gets someone else's card. Have people find the person with their card and introduce themselves. Variations: write down a fact, such as occupation, age, high school, or home state.

Guess. Play "What's My Line?" and have class members guess each person's occupation. Variations: home state, neighborhood, make of car.

Get to know an object. Bring a bag of potatoes to class. Give each person a potato. Have everyone "get to know" the potato, and then introduce the potato to another person, or to the rest of the class. Throw all the potatoes into a pile, and have the participants find their own potato. Variations: a fruit, such as a pear, that people can eat afterward; get to know a shoe, introduce it, throw in pile and blindfolded, find your shoe.

Physical introductions. With eyes closed, everyone walks around the room shaking hands and saying hello to the others. Variations: with eyes open, go around and introduce your back to every other person's back in the class; divide up into pairs, one person closes his fist and the other tries to get it open; bumper cars—hands at side, eyes closed, walk around until you bump into someone, then introduce yourself, and keep moving; introduce your feet to someone else, usually with everyone on his back on the floor and shoes off.

Fantasies. People write a famous name on a piece of paper and pin it on someone else's back. Person tries to guess what name is pinned on his back. Variations: person "acts" or talks like his fantasy person while class or one other person tries to guess the person; participants talk about their fantasy person and why they admire the person or would like to be them.

Word associations. Ask your participants to write down what comes to mind when you hear the word "renaissance," or some other word. Then share the thoughts with another person. Variations: use a word that introduces the subject matter; do the association game orally.

Group exercises. Divide the class into several groups. Hand out puzzle pieces and have each group together try to put the puzzle in order. Variations: some of the puzzle pieces are in another group, and groups have to trade for one or two puzzle pieces. Create something. Divide into groups and pass out ordinary office supplies or objects to each group (like pencils, paper clips, or rubber bands). Ask each group to discuss, manipulate, and create a design of human nature with the objects. Have groups look at the other designs and explain the symbolism. Variations: create a design with tinker toys, playing cards, watercolors, or crayons.

Devices and Aids

Devices and teaching aids are props to help you present the material in an interesting, clear, or different manner. They help in elucidating the topic and in making your presentation more interesting.

Although these devices can help stimulate your group, don't overuse them. They should not be used as gimmicks and should not be used when something simpler or more direct communicates better. Also, there is nothing more devastating to the flow and message of your presentation than to have the technology break down. Be sure the equipment is set up properly, is functioning, and is timed to complement the rest of the session.

Here are just some of the devices that can help your teaching. Without becoming a media hype, feel free to mix and match them, using different aids in your sessions.

Chalkboard. In 1841 Josiah Bumstead wrote, "The inventor or introducer of the blackboard deserves to be ranked among the greatest benefactors to learning and science, if not among the greatest benefactors of mankind."[7] Although perhaps overstated, the chalkboard is a standard and helpful tool in learning. It is easy to use, and it can be erased quickly. The disadvantages of the chalkboard are that it is sometimes difficult to see, and the chalkboard also may be unpleasantly associated with more formal school days.

Flip chart. Sometimes called "the adult blackboard," the flip chart is a good alternative to the chalkboard. The flip chart may be easier to see and is more visually pleasing when different colors of markers are used. You can prepare some flip charts ahead of time, saving class time in writing and drawing.

Overhead projector. You can write on a transparency in class to enlarge your letters; prepare colored graphs and charts to illustrate points; and even spice a presentation with cartoons and homemade illustrations. Transparencies are inexpensive, easy to use, and can be used repeatedly. You can get fancy in your transparencies as well.

Slides. If you want to use the illustrations more than once, slides are a good way to achieve clarity and color. You can also make your own homemade slides simply and inexpensively.

Films and slide shows. There are thousands of films and slide shows on just about every topic imaginable, and many of them are free or low-cost from your public library, extension office, or from companies promoting various products. A good film or slide show is an asset to a presentation. Several film catalogues are available. Consult your local librarian for guides.

Videotapes. An alternative to films, videotapes are also particularly effective when you make one using your class as the "actors." Videotaping an interview, project or other class activity involving your participants gives them an unusual chance to see themselves and learn from themselves. Check into institutions or businesses that rent the equipment.

Records, cassettes, tapes. Good for short interludes for music, drama, or speeches. Sometimes hearing the "original" has more of an effect on listeners than having you reread the material.

Television. Either watching a live show or seeing a rerun together can be a good stimulus for group discussion and for seeing the television medium as an educational tool in everyday life.

Charts and graphs. Good for illustrating data, statistics, figures, and comparisons.

Other instructional aids you might want to consider are models, mock-ups, specimens, puppetry, cork boards, flannel boards, radio, and eight-millimeter movies.

Three good references for using audio-visual aids in your class are:

1. *AV Instruction: Technology, Media and Methods* (5th ed.), J.W. Brown, R.B. Lewis, and F.E. Harcleroad. New York: McGraw–Hill, 1977.
2. *Instructional Media and the New Technologies of Instruction*, Carlton W.H. Erickson, and David H. Curl. New York: Macmillan, 1972.
3. *Planning and Producing Audiovisual Materials*, (3rd ed.), Jerrold E. Kemp. New York: Thos. Y. Crowell, 1975.

Reading Lists, Handouts and Other Paper Chases

There are many stories of the teacher who shows up for the first class of a 10 session course with a list of 10 books for the class to read. With a full work day and other obligations, most adults would be likely to read one book in ten weeks. Yet, literature has been a big part of learning for most of us, and we want to convey the "classics" or have participants do some reading.

For many classes outside reading may be completely unnecessary. For other classes, you may be able to convey ideas and concepts through audio-visual methods rather than the print medium.

Where outside reading is advantageous, you can make it easier for your students to do the reading by:

1. Limiting the reading list to one book, preferably a paperback.
2. Recommending chapters of a book, or copying chapters of a book, following copyright laws, for your students.
3. Finding appropriate pamphlets and booklets.
4. Using articles from magazines.
5. Constructing your own summaries of longer works.

Although there may be some resistance to outside reading materials, there is considerably less to materials handed out in class. Some learners enjoy receiving lots of handouts although you should select carefully the type and number of handouts as well. Handouts can be used both in the class session and at home.

Decide how you want to use your handouts. Various handouts are used to provide information that would take too long to cover in class. Other handouts are added or supplementary material. Some are outlines of major points so participants don't have to spend time taking notes and can concentrate instead on what you are saying.

Be sure to time your handouts so that students are not looking over the papers while you are trying to get their attention. Sometimes handouts are given out just after a particular section has been covered, before the break, or at the end of class.

Items you may want to use as handouts include information briefs, summaries, study guides, publications, pamphlets, newspapers, magazines, articles, drawings, charts, illustrations, and annotated reading lists.

Another way to involve your students with print material in and out of class is with exercises. Paper exercises engage your participants in the learning process and keep them active and alert in class. They also are a nonjudgmental way of instructing and testing because the participant is not competing with anyone else. And paper exercises can be taken home and used for further reference. Paper exercises help people learn, and they break up the class and make it more interesting. Some kinds of paper exercises are worksheets, manuals, workbooks, puzzles, crossword puzzles, and quizzes and tests.

Out-of-Class Experiences

In adult learning the community can be your classroom. Resources abound in your community, and they can be tapped for a more stimulating and enriching course.

Here are some ideas.

- If guest speakers cannot come to you, go to them. Having them talk in their own work place or surroundings will be more enjoyable, too.
- Have the class do investigative work in your local library.
- Go on a field trip in or out of town to a factory, worksite, office, or company related to the subject you are studying.
- Visit a museum or local exhibition.
- Attend a meeting of a citizen's group, community action group, club, or organization working with the problem you are discussing.
- Conduct a class or two in a "nonclass setting," such as a park, restaurant, or tavern, as a way of stimulating a different and more open kind of discussion.
- Take advantage of conventions, conferences, and other gatherings happening in your area during the time of your session.
- Send class members out to interview media people, business leaders, workers, ministers, or other people associated with the topic you are studying.

Small Group Activities

Using intragroup activities can enhance your teaching in many ways. The activities will give your participants a different perspective on the topic, allow them to act in different "roles," and engage in discussion. Interaction with other participants leads to greater learning and provides creative breaks to stimulate your students.

There are countless ways to involve your participants, each with a slightly different twist and each one appropriate to a certain kind of topic or learning environment. Experiment with one or more even if you have never tried or even heard of them before.

In designing the experiences, mentally preview them yourself beforehand to simulate what might occur and what you need to set them up. Most of these exercises cannot be completed in ten or fifteen minutes. Allow time to divide into groups, introduce the concept and develop it, have closure, and time to become a class again.

Here are some common and uncommon ways to enhance your class.

Brainstorming. As a class, or in groups, people try to generate a wide variety of ideas, suggestions, and possibilities. In brainstorming, one is not allowed to criticize or evaluate an idea or suggestion. Usually all of the ideas are written down, and later distilled, compared, or used by the entire group. The object is to fantasize, break down barriers, elicit a variety of ideas from every person in the group.

Role playing. Two or more class members act out a real or hypothetical situation, usually taking roles not normally associated with that person. The object is to see the situation from another's perspective.

Case incidents. Analyzing a real life situation or case incident, different class members assume different positions on the issue in raising pros and cons.

Committee. The class breaks into or forms a committee to decide policy, study, or formulate ideas on a given topic. A position paper or list of recommendations may be the outcome.

Sensitivity group. Members of the group engage in various sensitivity exercises designed to bring out feelings and share experience with each other in a new way. For types of sensitivity exercises, see *Sense Relaxation: Below Your Mind*, by Bernard Gunther, New York: Collier Books, 1968.

Task force. The group engages in a specific mission trying to accomplish a given task. The task force then reports back to the rest of the class on progress and achievement.

Panel. Class members are chosen to engage in a discussion in front of the rest of the class, usually with one person serving as moderator. The panel format brings out different viewpoints and encourages discussion without taking sides.

Debate. Unlike a panel, a debate is designed to take sides and bring out opposite viewpoints. Usually with teams of two to four members each, participants present and then argue the pros and cons. A vote can be taken to choose the winning team if desired.

Interview. One or two members of the class can invite a guest speaker to be interviewed. Usually the interviewers prepare specific questions for the speakers to answer, and sometimes questions are taken from the rest of the class as well. This is a good way to use outside resources without listening to a speech.

Listening team. Dividing the class into groups of three—a speaker, a listener, and an observer. One person relates his or her experiences or ideas on the topic to another person, with the listening person questioning, repeating, and restating key phrases for clarification. The third person observes the entire process, and after a time limit, reports to the other two on what he observed. The people then shift roles and repeat so each person has a chance to be speaker, listener and observer.

Network group. The network group is made up of class members who meet together from time to time, either scheduled or not, to talk about a specific topic or simply to share problems.

Reaction panel. A small number of class members react to a talk, film, or other presentation with their observations. The goal is to get a critical review and class input.

Teaching Techniques. For Further Reading:
1. *Adult Learning in Your Classroom*, Edited by Philip G. Jones. Minneapolis: Training Magazine, 1982.
2. *Helping Adults Learn and Change*, by Dr. Russell L. Robinson. Milwaukee: Omnibook, 1979.
3. *Choosing Techniques for Teaching and Learning*, Hazel Taylor Spitze. Washington, D.C.: Home Economics Education Association, 1979.

Chapter 9
Making It Better—
Evaluations

"Most of the shadows in this life are caused by standing in one's own sunshine."

—Unknown

"I am an excellent teacher. I'm the best," she said. She said it, her students said it, former students said it, the schools where she taught said it. But something was wrong.

She was a professional dancer, and a professional dance instructor. She had trained at the Arthur Murray studios. She had spent 10 years in the Far East as a professional belly dancer, and when she returned to Denver, she began teaching professionally at several different schools. "I can teach anything," she said. And it was true. One time a couple needed to know how to dance a minuet. Elaine has seen it performed one time on a late night television movie, and taught it to them. But there was something wrong with her class in dance.

It wasn't her first class. She had taught scores, maybe hundreds of classes before. But the students were restless. They were complaining. And she was uncomfortable, too. She began to talk about her students, how they didn't respect her, didn't dress for class very well, didn't look right.

So the school administrator, Tracy Dunning, decided to find out what was wrong with the class, and to make it better. After talking with both Elaine and the students, she discovered that

Elaine had certain expectations of her students, in particular, their appearance and dress. Some chewed gum. The women did not wear dresses. And the students unconsciously felt Elaine's unhappiness, and so they became restless and unhappy as well.

Tracy solved the problem by having Elaine write down her expectations of the students—no gum chewing, proper dress, and so on. And before the next class, Elaine went over her expectations with the students. Fortunately, she explained them humorously rather than citing them as "rules," and so the students then knew what to expect, and could act accordingly.

Most classes do not get that kind of attention, that kind of help, and thus too many classes are not improved when they could be. But Elaine Norona recognized not only that even good teachers need help every once in a while, but also that "evaluation" can be nonthreatening and improve one's class. And Tracy Dunning was a good administrator, recognizing that most problems in classes for adults can be solved. By asking the students to help, and by working to solve the problem, together they made it a better class.

All teachers, even the best ones, can improve their teaching. You can revise your class, and do it in a way that says you are a good teacher. Evaluations are the first step in enhancing your class. They are a nonthreatening, easy, positive way to get feedback from your participants. An evaluation is not a report card. It is friendly suggestions, ideas, and hints from people who will be pleased that you asked them.

Too often people do evaluations because they think it is traditional, a formality, an exercise to do and get out of the way. "We're supposed to do them," said one teacher. But why? In this chapter we will explore how to make your class better by doing an evaluation, be it simple or more structured.

Every class is evaluated, even if it is simply an impression in the mind of each participant. An evaluation is meant to help the participants, teacher, and administrators realize what the strong and weak points of the class are so that the learning experience can be even better. An evaluation brings to light what is good in the class, as well as what can be done better. The class is evaluated not just on the basis of how well the teacher is doing, but also the interaction of the participants and the assistance of any administrators involved.

You Can Evaluate Yourself

You can evaluate yourself as a teacher. Author Russell Robinson offers two ways in which to evaluate yourself. One is by "habitual but unorganized introspection," or just sitting down and thinking about what you are doing. Another way is to rate your own performance by means of a list of questions or items you deem most important in your teaching and subject matter.[1]

A good time to evaluate yourself is immediately after the class ends. When you're alone, review what went on during the class, what went right, what went wrong or could be improved, and how you can change the next class to be better.

Other Teachers Can Evaluate You

Other teachers or an administrator can help improve your teaching. Someone can observe your class, and make comments afterward. You can observe another teacher's class, a person you respect, and get ideas. Or you can just approach another teacher outside of the classroom situation, and interview him. Ask some general questions, or ask about a specific problem you are having.

Participant feedback is the best way to evaluate your class. Your students are not only the consumers of your learning experience, and thus the ultimate judges, but also the best ones to complete the evaluation. They are the learners. If they are not learning as well as they could be, it does not matter what an outsider, another teacher, or an administrator might say. Outside observers, other teachers, and an administrator might all have helpful things to say. But it is the students who are in the best position to do the evaluation. Because they are the learners. And the success of the class depends upon their learning. Participant feedback is the best way to improve the quality of your class.

The participants can provide reactions to three aspects of the class: 1. the administration; 2. the teacher; 3. the participants themselves. It takes all three aspects to make a good class, including involved participants. As self-directed learners, your students should realize that they have some responsibility for the success of the class as well. It is their responsibility to see that they learn, and to help improve the class to make that happen.

There are several legitimate reasons why adult learning classes are evaluated:

    A. Overall, to find out how the class is doing.

    B. To weed out a very poor teacher.

    C. To improve the teacher and the class.

    D. To provide data to tell others about the class.

    E. As a synthesis of learned material.[2]

For you, the teacher, there is only one good reason to evaluate your class: To improve yourself as the teacher and to enhance the class.

An evaluation can be done at the last session of the class or while the course is still going on. It should be simple, and as short as possible. Ask questions you really want answered. An evaluation can be informal, or it can be structured with a written questionnaire. Evaluating can be done in three different ways.

Unstructured evaluation. Just talk informally about the class, with either an individual participant or the class as a whole. What did people like, what did they not like?

Directed evaluation. Write a list of specific questions you want answered. Ask the participants to respond orally as a group to each question.

Structured evaluation. A formal evaluation questionnaire can be designed and each participant fills out the questionnaire or writes a few paragraphs in essay form.

How To Do An Evaluation

1. Decide what things are important to you, and what questions to ask of your participants.
2. Decide, again before the class starts, how to do the evaluation—informally, as a group discussion, or as an individual questionnaire.
3. Decide when to do the evaluation—during the session or at the last class.
4. After you have the evaluations, compile the results. Write down not only the most frequently repeated comments, but also the ones that "hit you" the most. Be sure to notice the positive comments, what you did right, as well as what you did wrong.
5. Show others the results. Ask other people—teachers you admire, other teachers you know, the administrator of the pro-

gram—what the evaluations say and what they think.

6. Act upon the results. This cannot be stressed enough. An evaluation is just the first step in improving your class. Find out how to improve your teaching. Get ideas from literature or recommended readings. Get help from other teachers.

7. Follow up with your participants. Return to the participants and ask them for clarification on their comments, or ways in which you can improve your teaching. Again, you can do this as a group, individually, or just with one or two individuals whom you respect the most.

8. Experiment and change. Try to follow the recommendations by experimenting with a new technique or approach. Keep trying. Keep evaluating. Keep improving.

There is no one way to do an evaluation, and creativity, and imagination can pay off just as much in evaluation as in every other aspect of teaching adults. For example, teacher Susan Warden hands out a blank sheet of paper to each student at the end of the course. The students can write anything they want on it. To give them some guidance, she suggests topics they might want to comment on, or highlights particular questions she has about the class. But the students are free to comment on any aspect they want.

"It works very well," she says. "Students not only comment on negative aspects of the class, but on positive ones too, and that is very reassuring."

Warden also occasionally gets a few sincere but irrelevant comments on her evaluations, but that is to be expected. One of her favorites is the student who wrote, "I really like what you wore to class."

When To Do An Evaluation—
Before, During and After

Before. Teachers often don't think about evaluations until the end of the course, and even chapters about evaluations come at the end of books, but the time to think about evaluation is before the class starts. You need not construct the entire evaluation, but if you wait until the end of the course, it may be too late to do the kind of evaluation you want, or ask the kind of questions you want answered. Here are some things to think about before the class starts.

—What are the important aspects of my teaching I want evaluated?

—How do I want to do an evaluation—in conversation, as a group, with a questionnaire?

—When do I want to evaluate my teaching—as the class is progressing so that I can change it and make the class better even while I am teaching it, or after the course is over?

In particular, if you want to do a performance-related evaluation, in which you are rated on specific skills and behaviors, then you need to construct the evaluation beforehand to determine what constitutes a successful experience and what doesn't.

During. You can actually conduct an evaluation while the class is going on, change or modify some of the aspects of the class, and improve your class during the course. This kind of evaluation is often called formative evaluation.

A formative evaluation can be conducted midway through the course, or as early as the end of the first session. At the end of the first session, you might want to ask participants individually how they enjoyed the first session and what they might like to see as the course progresses. Or you might want to structure it into the actual class by having all group members discuss briefly what they would like to learn, thus generating ideas about what they would like to take place, what went on during the first class, and so on.

In doing a formative evaluation, be sure to follow up on your results and change the course to meet the needs of the participants better. One advantage of the formative evaluation is that you will discover the opinions and reactions of those students who might drop out before the end of the course, and those reactions might be valuable.

After. The most common time to do an evaluation is at the end of the course. It sums up how well the class did, and is thus often referred to as a summative evaluation. It can tell you how well you did, but it is too late—this time—to make any improvements or changes. It is useful in helping you to prepare for your next course, or simply to provide feedback to you on your strong and weak points—as a speaker, leader, helper—points which are important in your daily living, whether teaching or not.

In fact, we too infrequently have the opportunity for honest and positive feedback on our actions and behavior, and the adult learning situation is an excellent chance to get suggestions and ideas on helping yourself to improve your own image and behavior.

Constructing an Evaluation Questionnaire

Whether you are doing an unstructured evaluation (informally asking people what they liked and did not like), a directed evaluation (asking specific questions you want answers to), or a structured evaluation (a written individual questionnaire), the first thing to do is to determine a list of questions you want to ask, be they simply "How did it go?" or more complex and detailed questions. If you are doing your evaluation orally, you can then ask your participants, either individually or as a group, your questions. If you are going to have a written evaluation, here are the steps.

1. Review your list of questions. Have you asked everything you want answers to? Are the important questions there?
2. Group questions that are similar. Weed out questions that are repetitive or ask the same thing. Reword the questions that are not clear or could be better stated. Be careful not to have your question misinterpreted.
3. Design the questionnaire. The first consideration is to keep it short. One page is best, two pages maximum.
4. Decide which questions can best be answered in 'closed' questions and which questions can best be answered in 'open-ended' questions.

A closed question asks for an answer one of a few ways. Closed questions include true or false, yes or no, multiple choice, and ratings (on a scale of 1 to 5, or A to F). For example, a question about the facilities would best be asked as a closed question. "Were the facilities adequate? yes____ no____. If no, please comment _____." rather than asking the participant to write a paragraph on the facilities.

The type of closed question-and-answer format you use is also important. For some questions, such as, "Overall, were you satisfied with the course?" would best be answered in a yes/no format. On the other hand, some specifics about your teaching, such as, "How would you rate my ability to be clearly understood?", might be better on a scale of 1 to 5, thus giving you gradations of answers and an ability to perceive some distinctions and areas for improvement.

An open-ended question asks the respondent to write a paragraph or to make comments. The advantage of this form of question is that you may get some very good or original ideas and suggestions. The disadvantage is that people are less likely to fill out an open-ended question completely because it takes more work, time, and thought; whereas simple yes/no or 1-to-5 ranking is much easier to complete. Many questions could be phrased as either a closed question or an open-ended question, so make your choices wisely. Because your participants will not be able to answer many open-ended questions, make those the important questions where you want original responses.

Many questionnaires have both closed questions, usually at the beginning, and one to three open-ended questions at the end of the questionnaire, with instructions to use the other side of the paper if the respondent needs more space.

Following are typical questions to ask, examples of closed and open-ended questions and a sample evaluation questionnaire.

Sample Questions

How would you rate the instructor?

How would you rate the course?

How would you rate your experience?

Did the instructor have a good mastery of the subject matter?

Was the instructor well-prepared for the class?

Was the instructor's approach clear and organized?

Did the instructor make the goals and objectives clear at the beginning of the class?

Was the teacher able to communicate information?

Did the instructor stimulate discussion and involvement within the group?

Did the teacher meet the goals and objectives of the class?

Was the teacher friendly and personable?

More Specific Questions

Did the teacher:

Pace the course well and did not run out of time?

Use examples and illustrations to make points clearer?

Make efficient use of class time?

Usually hold your attention during class?

Be enthusiastic about teaching?

Stimulate you to discover new things on your own?

Make you feel comfortable to ask questions, disagree, and express your own opinion?

Discuss points of view other than his or her own?
Be fair and impartial in dealing with class members?
Stick to the point and not ramble?
Stimulate good group discussions?
Encourage quiet members to participate?
Encourage the class to get involved and participate in the direction of the course?

Closed Questions
Was the instructor adequately prepared?
Were missed classes rescheduled?
Were handouts/reading materials helpful?

Open-Ended Questions
What did you like about the class?
What didn't you like about it?
What suggestions or changes would you make?
What subject areas would you like to have seen included in the courses which were not covered?
What are the teacher's good points?
What areas of improvement does the teacher need?[3]

An evaluation of your course will help you, even if you are not teaching again. It is a positive way to get good suggestions for improving your teaching content and style, and the reactions by an overwhelming majority of your participants will be kind and helpful. Evaluate your course, and then follow up on the suggestions. It will make for a better course, and a better teacher.

Making It Better—Evaluations. For Further Reading:
1. *Idea Book for Designing More Effective Learning Activities*, by Waynne James and Phil Offill. Stillwater, Oklahoma: Oklahoma State University, 1979.

Chapter 10
Summary

When this author was in second grade, the teacher, Eileen Hargrove, put all assignments aside every Friday afternoon and read to us from the book, *Lazy Liza Lizard*. Ever since then, Friday has been my favorite day of the week, and I have fragmented memories of the joys of listening to Miss Hargrove read those stories.

About five years ago I decided to get a copy of *Lazy Liza Lizard* and reread those wonderful tales. The public library did not have it, the Bragg Elementary School library did not have it, even Miss Hargrove did not have it. After searching antique shops and rummage sales, I began embarrassing myself by asking every parent, children's librarian or publisher if they had ever heard of *Lazy Liza Lizard*. My mother, who runs a large used book sale every year, joined me in the search. She also wrote to rare book dealers around the country inquiring for me. Four years later a rare book dealer in Massachusetts sent the book, and I eagerly opened it up and read the first five stories.

To my immediate disappointment, they were all the same. Lazy Liza was not nearly so exciting a personality as I had recalled, and the book was quickly put down.

It was only then that it occurred to me that what made Lazy Liza so fascinating, what made Fridays my favorite day ever since 1955, was not the book, the reading, nor the day—but Miss Hargrove. She made those things come alive, and she was the reason I remembered them so well.

Like my second grade classroom, the most important thing in your class is you, the teacher. Ultimately, no media trick or interaction technique will make or break your class. You are the single most important link between your learners and what they want to learn. Your excitement, your pleasantness, your interest, enthusiasm, your enjoyment of the experience will make the difference for your participants. They will have gained something because of you. Hopefully, they will not have missed out on something because of you.

In this short book I have tried to put together the most successful practices now known in helping to teach adults. Whether you read the book, skimmed it, or even just glanced at it is not important. What is important is if you gained even one tip which will improve your class, making you a better teacher and helping your participants to learn more.

As we enter into the era of lifelong learning, it will become increasingly critical that each of us learn continually to keep up in our jobs, grow personally, and be better citizens. You can help in your role as a teacher. By viewing your teaching as a mutual sharing of ideas, experiences, and warmth, you can demonstrate that the best teacher is the one who continues to learn from his or her students. You can help make your class a rich, stimulating, and involving interaction: you can help make lifelong learning the same. The greatest of modern tragedies would be for lifelong learning to become homogenized, standardized, formalized, quantified, and unspontaneous.

One of the greatest joys in teaching is seeing the sparkle in someone's eyes, the delight in discovering something new, the warmth in making a new friend, establishing a new friendship, the opportunity to express oneself. You can join thousands of others in one of the exciting challenges of this century, helping to make us truly a nation of learners.

In the past hundred pages I attempted to show you how to plan better, teach, and improve your class. We talked about how adults learn, stressing the critical factors of self-image and past experiences, and how you can help your students learn better by listening, by helping insecure learners, by avoiding punishing actions, by providing supportive actions, and by adding a touch of humor.

In preparing your course, think about your goals, objectives, and methods for teaching, and put them into a time frame by making an outline for each class. Set a positive learning climate the first class meeting by getting to know the participants and having them get to know each other. If measurable outcomes are desired, define your terminal goals and relate your learning and testing to changes in behavior. Use your participants' experiences and knowledge throughout the class, and call on a variety of teaching techniques in assisting you to convey your message each time. Ask for critical feedback so you can improve your class for the next time, and use the feedback to improve yourself and your abilities.

Teaching adults is both a serious business and fun. I hope you enjoy it. And perhaps you will remain as alive and rich in your experience as the senior citizen I met in our building once.

One night at work I wearily went down to the basement to buy a soft drink from the vending machine. There I met an elderly man standing around, obviously waiting for an evening class to begin.

"Are you a student or the teacher?" I asked, not wanting to offend him either way. "Well, I suppose I'm the teacher, the man replied, "but I'm always learning too."

Appendix A
Writing Course Descriptions

If you are offering a course that will be publicized through a catalog or brochure, you or the course sponsor will need to write a course description. The course description is vital to getting people to enroll in your course. A good course description can mean many enrollments while a poor course description can doom your course before it starts. Ideally, you should work with your class sponsor in writing the course description. Find out if you can or should submit a course description, and then follow these guidelines.

Many if not most course descriptions are repetitive, dull or grammatically sloppy. If people do not read your course description, they will not take your course.

Look at a typical course catalog. See how many of the descriptions start out, "This class will . . ." or "The instructor will . . ." or "An introduction to . . ." These openers are uninformative and boring when used over and over again. Following a few simple rules, you can write a course description that is simple, interesting, clear and readable.

Many course descriptions are poorly written because they are:
1. dull
2. repetitive
3. sloppy
4. uninformative
5. too casual
6. too complex.

Here are some poor course description sentences.

"Course goals are to learn the basics of Native American beadwork." (dull)

"Lee wishes to present his interpretation of oriental philosophies of life and world views. He hopes that it would serve as a mirror to help you understand and appreciate your own culture better. Lee is a perennial student of learning," (teacher, not course, oriented)

"Bring your own lunch, spend a relaxed hour with some great ideas, great thinkers and excellent presenters." (too casual)

"Bring your own stories. We will relate stories which have a personal meaning to us. Stories may be either from history or experience. We will pursue what our stories mean for life and faith." (repetitive)

"This is an opportunity for you to get some challenging experience and to meet new faces." (uninformative)

The course description is made up of these items:

A. The title
B. Logistics
C. Course description
D. Teacher biography

The title. The title should be simple or catchy. Long or complex titles tend to confuse, and dull titles will not capture the reader's eye. Generally, for skill classes such as home repair or the arts you will want a simple title. For idea classes such as interpersonal relations and social issues catchy titles will attract the reader, turning an average or dull topic into an interesting one. Here are some good course titles.

"Stained Glass" (simple)

"101 Uses for a Dead Poet" (catchy)

Logistics. Logistics include the teacher's name, class location, day, length, cost, material fees, course number and other adjunct information. The course sponsor normally provides this information, although you should be aware of all information pertinent to your class.

The course description. Every course description should have these elements:

—it should be enticing or interesting
—it should be factually complete and accurate
—it should have solid course information

Every newspaper story has to have the 5 W's in the first two paragraphs—Who, What, Where, When, Why. Your job in writing a course description is much easier, since Where and When are in the logistics section, and Who is irrelevant or a useless gesture (don't write, "Everyone should take this course.")

Here are a few guidelines for the description.

1. The description should run from 30 words to 120 words in length. Fewer than 30 is too sketchy, more than 120 is too long.
2. The description should be divided into two paragraphs if it is

over 60 words. More than 60 words in one paragraph is too hard to read.

3. The teacher biography or qualifications should not be mixed in with the course description.

4. Do not use abbreviations unless EVERYONE knows what they stand for.

5. Write in complete sentences. Incomplete sentences should be used infrequently and only for emphasis.

Your description should focus around the content of the course or the learner, not around the course itself or you as the teacher. To attract learners, the description should emphasize the benefits to the learner coming from either the results of attending the course, or from the value of the subject matter itself. Learners are interested in themselves and in the content of the course, not in the course itself or the teacher.

In general, the first one or two sentences should be enticing, dramatic or otherwise interesting. The following two to five sentences should be a summary of the scope and content of the course.

The first five words of the description will often determine if the reader will go on or pass to another course description.

Here are six good opener techniques:

1. A definition
2. The end result
3. The outstanding or impressive fact
4. A question
5. The quotation
6. The distraction

Definitions, end results and impressive facts are used frequently in course descriptions. Questions, quotations or distractions are used sparingly.

Here are some poor openers:

"The aim of this course is to . . ." (course oriented)

"Shirley has been teaching ballet for two years now . . ." (teacher oriented)

"This class will . . ." (focus on course)

"The teacher will explain . . ." (focus on teacher)

Here are some good openers:

"Batik is an age old art of fabric colouring using wax and dye." (Definition)

"Effective fiction enables the reader to live a story as if it's his or her own life." (End result)

"You can be a moral person without following traditional religions." (End result)

"Baffled, bored or intimidated by Opera?" (The question)

"Lighting is the key to all photography." (Outstanding fact)

" No man is an island.' " (Quotation)

"Does your life seem like a soap opera?" (A question)

"Grr. Hold it Horace! Don't throw that pillow yet." (Distraction)

"Fred Astaire, Ginger Rogers, Gene Kelly—And you." (content and end result, excellent enticer)

Following your opener you can talk about what will be covered in the course and other content matter. While you should avoid the following sentence first words in the first two sentences of the opener, they are appropriate for the rest of the description IF they are not repeated in the same description.

Sentence first words:

"We will spend time . . ."

"We will . . ."

"Here's your chance to . . ."

"Learn . . ."

"Topics covered . . ."

"Included are . . ."

"The class . . ."

"This course . . ."

"These questions . . ."

"Participants will . . ."

"We will explore . . ."

"The course is designed . . ."

"The aim of this course . . ."

"Find out about . . ."

Don't use useless or meaningless sentences, such as "Time allowing we will discuss other areas."

The teacher biography. The teacher biography should be 15 to 50 words in a separate paragraph underneath the course description. Some organizations run all of their teacher biographies at the end of the catalog.

The biography should have two seemingly contradictory goals —1) to establish you as qualified; 2) to project your image as a peer, not too far above the potential learners. Learners want to know you are qualified, but they also want someone who can relate to them.

Your qualifications should be stated in terms of experience. Use credentials or degrees only as a last resort. By including your interest or motivation in teaching the course, the participants will also see you as a likeable peer.

Here are examples of good course descriptions.

Batik

Batik is an age old art of fabric colouring using wax and dye. This workshop is open to beginning and advanced students. It covers preparation of cloth and dyes, some design principles and sources, effects of different wax techniques and mixtures, colour theories related to the craft, and the various finishing methods. Individual attention will be emphasized. Students can expect to complete four to six works.

Political Advertising

The battlefield is the minds of American voters—and the ultimate weapon is television. With each election video politics has become more and more a prevailing force in American government.

Gary Yordan will present some examples of political advertising and the strategy and methods used in developing the ads.

Why Are There Mountains?

Why are there mountains, anyway. Why did the old earth go to all the trouble? Why doesn't the whole planet look like Nebraska? We will examine the revelations of plate tectonics and explore the old and new theories of mountain formation. We will also take a Kodachrome journey to the Himalayas. Depending on class wishes, a field trip may be scheduled.

Do I Choose Motherhood?

The "biological clock" ticks away, causing a sense of urgency in many women to decide or re-examine their decision to bear a child, "before it is too late." This class sheds light on what remains of a hazy, mystical area to many women. There is no right or wrong in this class. Come explore your own solutions in a warm, supportive group of women.

99

Appendix B
Promoting Your Own Class

Every course needs promotion. While the course sponsor is responsible for publicizing your course and getting enrollments, you can assist your course sponsor in promoting your class and making it even more successful.

Before promoting your course, you should talk with the sponsor and work with the administrators in promotion. Discuss your ideas and make sure they approve of your promotion plans before proceeding. But given that the sponsor is well informed, most administrators encourage their teachers to promote their own classes.

There are four basic types of promotion available: 1) word of mouth; 2) printed materials; 3) the media; and 4) special events.

Word of mouth

Word of mouth is the most effective means of promoting your course. Tell colleagues, friends, business associates, and community leaders about your course.

The easiest way to let others know about your course is to send them the catalog with your course in it, along with a note calling attention to your course and the page number where it can be found.

You can also make an announcement at a meeting. Do not be concerned about being too egotistical about announcing your own activities. Most people will be appreciative of the information, and pass it along to others. By informing your colleagues and friends you may be announcing your course to those most interested in attending.

Printed materials

Flyers. Amidst all the advertising, activities, and events going on, people may not have been able to see your course description in a catalog. By inexpensively printing up a flyer and mailing it to highly selective lists of people most likely to enroll, you can gain attention for your course.

Flyers can be composed inexpensively with a typewriter, press type, or rub on letters, and supplemented with line art drawings.

Typesetting costs more but might be worth it depending on your audience and the number of flyers you are printing. One page flyers can be printed inexpensively at quick print shops or even reproduced at copy centers. The standard flyer is one page, both sides, printed on colored stock and folded twice to fit into a regular envelope.

One page flyers can be distributed to select places for people to pick up, such as the public library or centers where people interested in your subject frequent. They can also be mailed to highly selective lists of people most likely to attend. Leaders, club members, and past participants in classes are good to mail to.

Posters. In some communities, such as university towns or rural resort areas, posters are a major and accepted way of communicating. If this is the case in your area, posters can be an effective and inexpensive method of getting the word out. Quite simply, if there are bulletin boards established in stores and community centers, then posters are effective. If you do not see a lot of bulletin boards and other posters in your area, then posters probably are not very effective.

Posters can be printed very inexpensively at a quick print shop or a copy center. But they should be attractive. Your poster should have a headline in large letters to get the reader's attention, followed by a short explanation of the course and where to get full information or register. Make it simple. A poster reader can only copy down a phone number or address, so make your instructions very clear and simple. For example, "To register, call the Community Services Office at 987-6543." A simple drawing clipped out of a magazine or a line drawing will help make your poster stand out in a crowd, as will printing it on colored paper.

Doing Mass Mailings. Mass mailings can either be very effective or a big waste of money. It is dependent on the specificity of your mailing list and the cost involved. As with some military recruiting, the philosophy of a mailing list is to get a "few good names."

For example, a residential mailing list rented from a mailing list company would probably be a poor investment, because: a) it covers all residents and is not very specific or narrow in focus; and b) it is generally expensive. A large residential mailing list of 5,000 names would cost you over $1,000 to mail.

On the other hand, a small but well chosen list that is low priced can be very effective. For example, if you are teaching a course on Stress Management in the Workplace, you could ask the Chamber of Commerce, Rotary Club, and Jaycees for their membership lists. If they would comply and give you their lists for no charge, it would be very worthwhile to mail to those lists.

Since the list would be smaller, say only 1,000 names, you can label the flyers yourself and save money. The business list will also have a higher return rate, since those people would be the most interested in your topic.

Thus, if you can get a list of even a few names of people concerned about the topic you are teaching, it can be very worthwhile. But just mailing your flyer to people without a known interest in your subject area is probably a waste of time and money.

Publicity

The most effective avenue for getting participants for your class is probably the media—newspapers, radio, magazines, and television. Just about any teacher of any topic can seek publicity, and the sponsor of your class will probably be delighted if you receive publicity for your course because it means publicity for the sponsor's total program as well. Unlike advertising, publicity costs no money and can yield as high or even higher results than paid advertising. You can approach your local media on one of these bases: A) your class is 'news,' interesting, human interest to their readers, viewers, or listeners; or B) your class is a community or public service that will help their readers or viewer audience.

As News. Media people are always looking for stories that are unusual, current, or of human interest. They will be more than glad to feature you in a story if there is a news value to it. Two things to remember: media people are interested in an unusual slant or approach; and they are interested in the story, not in your course.

To receive media attention, you have to give the media a different slant or approach that makes your course stand out from the crowd. The slant is usually either because the subject is different or you as the teacher are different.

Some subject slants: your course has never been offered before; it is very popular these days; it is unusual; it is fun; it appeals to a certain kind of person.

Some teacher slants: you are new to town; an expert on the topic; new to the topic; very young; very old; you have written on the topic; you acquired your knowledge in an interesting way.

By thinking up a new angle on your course, you can turn an ordinary course into a 'news event,' based on some difference in your course that makes it different from all the others.

Here are the major media to promote your course:

Newspapers. Call up the city editor or a reporter you know and give them your 'angle' or how your course is unique. Ask them if they would like to do a feature on it. If they are not interested, you can always write a three or four paragraph story yourself, making it short and stressing your angle, and send it in. Often a newspaper has small amounts of space to fill on a page, and uses "filler" stories, short articles of just one or two paragraphs. If your story is short, it could go on a good page and even a two paragraph story will be seen by thousands of people.

Remember a newspaper has many different sections to it. There is local news, sports, financial page, family lifestyle (or the women's page) and features. So your story may be of particular interest to an editor of one of these specialized sections.

Radio. Radio stations offer news, news announcements, interviews, and public service announcements. When writing up a news announcement, make it short—one paragraph, two at the most. The announcement will be read as part of the local news, or as filler in between regular programming. Many radio stations have interview programs, and if your topic is suitable to that format, it is well worth your while. Radio stations look for topics of personal interest to listeners, such as interpersonal relationships, travel items, how-to skills, and home skills.

Public service announcements, or PSAs, are designed as a community service by radio and television stations. If your course is sponsored by a nonprofit organization, or is given free, your course is eligible. Just write up a ten second, twenty second, or thirty second announcement and send it in. As the station receives many requests for PSAs, they will probably be unable to tell you if and when it will be on the air.

Television. Like radio, television has news announcements, interviews, and public service announcements. The difference with television is that they are interested in something visual. If you are doing something that involves a good visual picture, such as cooking, arts and crafts, or a course out of doors, a television station might be interested.

While not guaranteed, seeking publicity from your local media does not take a lot of time, and money for only a few postage stamps, and is well worth the effort. If your course is run on the local media, you can gain many participants for your course.

Advertising. Occasionally, sponsors will advertise your class in the local newspaper. It is rare that a single course would be advertised on radio or television, as those media are very expensive. A newspaper ad would most likely be a small spot ad of one to eight inches, one or two columns wide. If you feel that an ad would be an effective way to promote your class, discuss it with your sponsor. The best day to run an advertisement is Sunday, and the effectiveness of a single ad will be known three days later, as any reader will register or call for more information within a two to three day time period.

It is worth your time, and perhaps a little money, to promote your own class. You know better than anyone the likely audience for your class, and you will benefit from higher attendance.

Bibliography

Apps, Jerold W., *The Adult Learner on Campus*, Follett Publishing Company: Chicago, 1981.

Bischof, Ledford J., *Adult Psychology*, Harper & Row, Publishers: New York, 1969.

Block, Linda K., "Teaching Adults in Continuing Education," University of Illinois: Champaign, 1979.

Brevard County Public Schools, "Adult/Community Education: A Quick and Handy Guide for Teachers," School Board of Brevard County: Rockledge, Florida, 1979.

The College Board, *Lifelong Learning During Adulthood*, The College Board: New York, 1978.

Cross, K. Patricia, *Adults As Learners*, Jossey-Bass Publishers: San Francisco, 1981.

Dickinson, Gary, *Teaching Adults: A Handbook for Instructors*, General Publishing Co. Limited: Don Mills, Ontario, 1973.

Draves, William A., *The Free University: A Model for Lifelong Learning*, Follett Publishing Company: Chicago, 1980.

Draves, William A., "Teaching Free: An Introduction to Adult Learning for Part Time Teachers," Learning Resources Network: Manhattan, Kansas 1976.

Draves, William A., "Course Evaluations," Learning Resources Network: Manhattan, Kansas, 1981.

Epstein, Joseph, Editor, *Masters: Portraits of Great Teachers*, Basic Books, Inc., Publishers: New York, 1981.

Freire, Paulo, *Pedagogy of the Oppressed*, Herder and Herder: New York, 1972.

Grabowski, Stanley M., *Training Teachers of Adults: Models and Innovative Programs*, Syracuse University: Syracuse, New York, 1976.

Gross, Ronald, Editor, *Invitation to Lifelong Learning*, Follett Publishing Company: Chicago, 1982.

Gross, Ronald, *The Lifelong Learner*, Simon & Schuster: New York, 1977.

Highet, Gilbert, *The Art of Teaching*, Vintage Books: New York, 1954.

Illich, Ivan, *Deschooling Society*, Harper & Row, Publishers: New York, 1970.

Ilsley, Paul, J., and Niemi, John, A., *Recruiting and Training Volunteers*, McGraw–Hill Book Company: New York, 1981.

James, Waynne, and Offill, Phil, *Idea Book for Designing More Effective Learning Activities*, Oklahoma State University: Stillwater, Oklahoma, 1979.

Kidd, J.R., *How Adults Learn*, Association Press: New York, 1973, 1959.

Knowles, Malcolm, *Self-Directed Learning*, Follett Publishing Company: Chicago, 1975.

Knowles, Malcolm, *The Adult Learner: A Neglected Species*, Gulf Publishing Company: Houston, 1973.

Knowles, Malcolm, *The Modern Practice of Adult Education*, Follett Publishing Company: Chicago, 1980.

Knox, Allen, Editor, *Teaching Adults Effectively*, Jossey–Bass Publishers: San Francisco, 1980.

Mills, H.R., *Teaching and Training: A Handbook for Instructors*, John Wiley & Sons: New York, 1977.

Nadler, Leonard, *Developing Human Resources*, Gulf Publishing Company: Houston, 1970.

NAPCAE, *A Treasury of Techniques for Teaching Adults*, NAPCAE: Washington, D.C., 1964.

NAPCAE, *Tested Techniques for Teachers of Adults*, NAPCAE: Washington, D.C., 1972.

NAPCAE, *When You're Teaching Adults*, NAPCAE: Washington, D.C., 1959.

NAPCAE, *The Second Treasury of Techniques for Teaching Adults*, NAPCAE: Washington, D.C., 1970.

National Association for Public Continuing and Adult Education (NAPCAE), *You Can Be a Successful Teacher of Adults*, National Association for Public Continuing and Adult Education: Washington, D.C., 1974.

Nelson, Florence, *Yes You Can Teach!* Carma Press: St. Paul, Minnesota, 1977.

Reimer, Everett, *School Is Dead*, Doubleday & Company: Garden City, New York, 1972.

Robinson, Russell D., *Helping Adults Learn and Change*, Omnibook Company: Milwaukee, 1979.

Smith, Robert M., *Learning How to Learn: Applied Theory for Adults*, Follett Publishing Company: Chicago, 1982.

Srinivasan, Lyra, *Perspectives on Nonformal Adult Learning*, World Education: New York, 1979.

Tough, Allen, *The Adult's Learning Projects*, The Ontario Institute for Studies In Education: Toronto, 1971.

Training Magazine, Adult Learning in Your Classroom, Training Books: Minneapolis, 1982.

Verduin, John R., Miller, Harry G., and Greer, Charles E., *Adults Teaching Adults*, Learning Concepts: Austin, Texas, 1977.

Wilson, Marlene, *The Effective Management of Volunteer Programs*, Volunteer Management Associates: Boulder, Colorado, 1976.

Notes

Chapter 2.
  [1]J. Roby Kidd, *How Adults Learn*, (New York, NY: Association Press, 1973, 1959), page 95.
  [2]Ronald Gross, *Invitation to Lifelong Learning*, (Chicago, IL: Follett Publishing Company, 1982), page 48.
  [3]Kidd, page 95.

Chapter 3.
  [1]Kenneth Eble, *The Craft of Teaching: A Guide to Mastering the Professor's Art* (San Francisco, CA: Jossey–Bass Publishers, 1976), page 13.
  [2]Florence Nelson, *Yes You Can Teach*, (St. Paul, MN: Carma Press, 1977) page 7.
  [3]Russell Robinson, *Helping Adults Learn and Change*, (Milwaukee, WI: Omnibook Company, 1979), page 50.
  [4]Robinson, page 52.
  [5]Ibid.
  [6]Robinson, page 56.
  [7]Nelson, page 30.

Chapter 4.
  [1]John R. Verduin, Harry G. Miller, and Charles E. Greer, *Adults Teaching Adults*, (Austin, TX: Learning Concepts, 1977) pages 84–88.
  [2]Robinson, page 86.

Chapter 5.
  [1]Verduin, et al, page 24.
  [2]Robinson, page 78.
  [3]Robinson, page 78.
  [4]H.R. Mills, *Teaching and Training: A Handbook for Instructors*, (New York, NY: John Wiley & Sons, 1977) page 97.
  [5]Waynne James, and Phil Offill, *Idea Book for Designing More Effective Learning Activities*, (Stillwater, OK: Oklahoma State University, 1979), page 143–144.

Chapter 6.

[1]Jerold Apps, *The Adult Learner On Campus*, (Chicago, IL: Follett Publishing Company, 1981) page 156.

[2]Nelson, pages 21-22.

[3]Apps, page 154.

[4]Nelson, page 24.

[5]Ralph Ruddock, "All Right On the Night—A Survival Kit for Absolute Beginners," *Adult Education (London)*, Volume 45, Number 3, 1972, page 145.

[6]Ruddock, page 144.

Chapter 7.

[1]Draves, "Teaching Free: An Introduction to Adult Learning for Part Time Teachers," (Manhattan, KS: Learning Resources Network, 1976), pages 12-13.

Chapter 8.

[1]Robinson, page 43 and Eble, pages 58-59.

[2]Nelson, page 13

[3]Nelson, page 14.

[4]Eble, pages 52-53.

[5]Eble, page 60.

[6]Robinson, page 97.

[7]C. Anderson, *Teaching in American Education, 1650-1900*, (Washington, D.C.: US Government Printing Office, 1952), page 18.

Chapter 9.

[1]Robinson, page 102.

[2]Draves, "Course Evaluations," (Manhattan, KS: Learning Resources Network, 1980), pages 1-4.

[3]Ibid.

INDEX